Hooked on Screens

How to Get Your 5-14 Year Old to Put Down the Phones, Video Games, and Electronic Devices and Pick Up a Book

By Dr. Colleen Carroll
#1 Bestselling Author

FREE BONUS QUIZ!

Is Your Child

Hooked on Screens?

http://bit.ly/screentimequiz

The mind is everything. What you think, you become.

Buddha

Website: www.innovativereading.com.

Email: drcarroll@innovativereading.com.

Ordering Information: Quantity sales. Special discounts are available on multiple purchases by corporations, associations, and others.

For details, contact the "Special Sales Department" at the email address above.

Hooked on Screens, Dr. Colleen Carroll--1st edition, 2018

www.evolveglobalpublishing.com

Book Layout: © 2017 Evolve Global Publishing

ISBN: 978-0-692-93909-3 (Paperback)
ISBN: 978-0-692-93912-3 (Hardcover)
ISBN-13: (Createspace)
ISBN-10: (Createspace)
ISBN: (Smashwords)
ASIN: (Amazon Kindle)   B071GPZXPP
This book is available on Barnes & Noble, Kobo, Apple iBooks (digital)

Hooked on Screens

Colleen Carroll

Table of Contents

Dedication

This book is dedicated to my wonderful husband, Dan.
May we spend many more incredible years reading together.

Accolades for Hooked on Screens

We are so grateful for Dr. Carroll's work helping families balance screen time with life. Screens aren't going away. In fact, even schools are requiring kids to use them more and more. It is imperative that families understand the importance of activities that don't involve screens to raise happy, healthy, well-rounded children. At our academy, we do this through music instruction. Dr. Carroll uses reading! These are skills that will stay with children for a lifetime. We advocate mindful use of technology to help with life, not take over life.

Claudia Huter and Dr. Steven Huter, Founder Directors, Larchmont Music Academy, www.LarchmontMusicAcademy.com, teaching over 750 students per year

Dr. Carroll's work is such an important component to healthy childhood development in the modern setting. Her capacity to help families see themselves and come up with workable solutions for a balanced approach to the use of screens is nothing short of miraculous in the transformation that occurs, for the child as well as the entire family.

Sarica Cernohous, Licensed Acupuncturist and Practitioner of Traditional Chinese Medicine, Author of The Funky Kitchen, Founder of naturallylivingtoday.com, Mom of two children ages 10 and 12

Visit www.InnovativeReading.com for free resources!

As the mother of two elementary-aged boys, I know first-hand how important it is to instill great reading habits. With all the distractions of technology today, it makes it difficult. That's why Dr. Carroll's work is so vital to our society! She has proven methods to help me help my kids, and what parent doesn't want that?

> *Pamela Zimmer, Author, Speaker, Mentor and "Self-Care Queen",*
> *www.PamelaZimmer.com, Mom of two boys ages 10 and 7*

Dr. Colleen Carroll has been a tremendous resource to families I work with as a parent educator. Her advice is helpful, reassuring and above all, actionable! Dr. Carroll's book, **Hooked on Screens**, is especially important today as our children are faced with psychological challenges from the negative effects of electronic devices. I highly recommend her work to families looking for answers that will help their children grow into responsible and kind adults.

> *Maria Dismondy, Award-winning Author and Parent Educator,*
> *www.MariaDismondy.com, Mom of three children ages 8, 5 and 3*

Advancements in digital technology, particularly mobile technology, are creating a generation of sedentary tech addicts. This addiction poses a danger to our children's physical and mental health. Dr. Carroll's work is a crucial step towards increased awareness of the dangers of digital addiction and will provide more people with the tools necessary to take action to prevent it. It is time to get kids to step away from their screens and get moving because, as we have witnessed at BOKS, active kids = active minds.

> *Nancy Day, Coordinator at Build Our Kids' Success, RI,*
> *www.bokskids.org, Mom of two children ages 10 and 14*

Visit www.InnovativeReading.com for free resources!

Studies have shown and experts and parents know – boys can often be very reluctant, stubborn, and adamantly AGAINST reading. (Video games and screens offer instant gratification, and are easy to learn!) Dr. Colleen Carroll provides the information you need to understand the reasons behind his fascination with screens, and then she gives you the practical strategies you MUST HAVE to move him from resistance of books to interest and enthusiasm. With her wisdom, experience, and expertise, she'll help you get your child unplugged from screens and plugged into reading!

Janet Allison, Author, Educator, Family Coach, and Founder of Boys Alive! www.boysalive.com Mom to two daughters, 29 and 31

In our digital world, distractions have become commonplace in the modern home. Kids spend their free time with devices and video games while reading gets pushed to the back burner. This is a disturbing trend and one that is unlikely to lead to our childrens' future accomplishments. Luckily, we have Dr. Carroll. She is committed to equipping parents with proven strategies that turn the tide back in our favor. The importance of her work cannot be overstated. Bottom line, her strategies work and will help your child move toward higher success.

Brent Basham, Co-Host www.DigitalDads.fm, Dad of three children ages 7, 9 and 12

As a career coach and the mother of two avid readers who successfully graduated college in four years, I affirm that reading expands knowledge and vocabulary which gives you confidence to have a personal and professional voice. Dr. Carroll's book, **Hooked on Screens**, will give your child a head start as a strong reader while minimizing the distraction and addiction of digital devices. I highly recommend Dr. Carroll *and* her book!

Juliet Murphy, Career Coach to Parents & High School Students, Speaker, Author: #WHAT'S NEXT AFTER HIGH SCHOOL? http://julietmurphy.com/   Mom of two children

As a foreign language teacher since 1984, with students from different countries ranging in ages from 8 to 80, I can attest that those who were successful in learning a second language almost always had one skill in common: they read well in their first language! As technology use has increased within my student population, difficulty and stress has also increased. Dr. Carroll's work will enable you to give your children a chance to be successful in their first language and any other subject they need to learn. My own two boys, brought up as the digital age began, were encouraged to read before using any screens. They love to read now, and their commendable grades and enjoyment of high school and college are a result of that time spent reading.

Laura Woford, Author of Art2Pray, Jumpstart Mental Focus Series, Artist and Spanish Teacher, Mom of two boys ages 17 and 19

Introduction: Welcome to Innovative Reading!

Hello Mom and Dad,

If you have been worried about how much your child is on a smartphone lately, or how many hours a day he's playing video games instead of playing outside or reading a book, then you've come to the right place.

These days, almost every child from the time he can walk throughout the teen years spends hours a day using technology. This book is about how parents can help break this cycle with their child before it's too late.

The negative effects of long-term electronic device use are becoming more obvious now that enough time to conduct research has gone by since the invention of the internet, video games and social media. The results are clear; kids are spending way too much time with their heads hung over their smartphones and iPads and not nearly enough time socializing with friends and family, playing (real) games and sports, or reading books.

I've read the research and done quite a bit of my own and believe me, it's not good. This book is not about all the negative effects, however. There are plenty of articles out there now on that. This book is what you can do to stop the problem of technology over-use in your home before it's too late.

Maybe you've already noticed a negative impact at home and that's why you are reading this. Perhaps you already feel a disconnect with your pre-teen due to the phone, or have found your child texting friends or on Snapchat when she should be sleeping. Maybe your son promises to do his homework but instead you find him playing Minecraft in his room with the bookbag still closed hours after dinner. Or it could be that you haven't gotten there yet but you'd like to avoid the inevitable arguments that scenarios like these cause in homes around the globe every single night.

If you have children in the modern world, this book is for you. I respectfully offer my very best ideas and strategies that have evolved over two decades of working with children and parents in education. They have been honed over time to create a unique system that works to ensure your child won't be forever hooked on screens.

I wish you and your family the happiness and satisfaction of real communication, time spent together and the wonderful experience of curling up with a good book.

Sincerely,

Dr. Colleen Carroll

Foreword

By Jonathan Christian

I'm the Chief Strategist at a company called We Make Stuff Happen and since 2009 I've been pretty much glued to my mobile device as I've taught businesses how to leverage the power of the internet through social media.

How interesting then that I get to write a foreword for my good friend, Dr. Colleen, about putting the device down. Now that might seem a little strange, but even I believe she's so right. I have, to my cost, spent way too much time with my head buried over the little screen in front of me rather than looking up and enjoying the people and events around me in real life. So, I can attest that her book has the most incredible value for parents and children in today's society.

Don't get me wrong, I believe in the benefits of social media, and I love my devices! I also believe they're the most valuable tools that we have in our modern world when used appropriately. But that doesn't mean the only way we should interact is through social media and devices. On the contrary, they should augment our interactions, and help us instead of hinder us.

Here is an example of what I mean by that. I remember the summer of 2012. I was working with a children's sleep away camp and the camp had not yet embraced social media (although of course the counselors did). So since this is my business, I encouraged them to set up their own social media accounts.

On Wednesday there were two "likes" on their Facebook page - myself and the program director. By Friday, they were just warming up to the idea of using social media when quite shockingly that afternoon we had a horrible and unexpected windstorm come through! In the space of twelve minutes, several hundred pine trees had either broken or been uprooted, right across this camp. As you can imagine, it was quite an unnerving experience for everyone.

The storm shut off all traditional forms of communication. It took out the electricity, the telephone wires had gone down, and there was no way of sharing information with people outside of the camp except through the Wi-Fi that I had on my cell phone and the camp's Facebook page. There were 130 sets of parents who had heard numerous rumors about the impact of the storm on the camp and were, of course, extremely worried about their children. Within two days, that page had gone from 2 likes to 865! We communicated critical messages in real time to concerned families about what had happened at camp, and successfully reunited all parents together with their children.

I am proud of how we handled that event and it highlights the positive potential of social media. But as a Dad of three teenage girls, I also REALLY get the value of putting *down* the phone. I get the value of authentic face time, not Apple FaceTime. I get the value of going outside and enjoying fresh air, of having family game nights, of not having the television on, of having text-free weekends, or as I often call it a "digital sabbatical". And that, my friends, is the beauty of this book.

Hooked on Screens gives you compelling logic about why you should put the smartphone down. There are wonderful modern-day examples of how to share quality family time with old-fashioned values. I recommend that you take the message to heart and use it for all it's worth, because Dr. Colleen has spent 20 years studying the dynamics of reading with children. She's also an expert in digital technology use and the advantages and disadvantages that it brings to the 21st century family.

So as the social media strategist, I encourage you to read this book (especially in paper version so you're not looking at a screen) apply the wisdom, and then share it widely so it can help other parents do the same.

Thanks so much, Dr. Colleen, for asking me to write the foreword. I truly believe that your work is a gift to humanity and I anticipate seeing you on the bestseller list!

Overview

Our son was showing signs of aggression and withdrawal as soon as he entered middle school. We thought maybe it was just the early teen years but we noticed it got worse as the use of his electronic gadgets increased. We had bought him a cell phone, and he also owned video games and a laptop. We learned from Dr. Carroll that screen time might be causing this behavior change and she gave us several suggestions of what we could do about it. Implementing changes at home was not easy! But we made a significant impact on our son's behavior with her recommendations, and we're all much happier for it. We can't thank her enough!

Tom and Myra N. Cincinnati, OH

Every day in the United States alone, millions of children spend hours glued to their screens playing video games, texting, involved in social media, and watching videos instead of participating in healthy activities that challenge their brains and improve their communication, social and behavioral skills, advance their intellect, challenge their bodies physically, or simply breathe fresh air and take in the sun.

These screens come in the form of cell phones (aka smartphones), tablets (like the iPad), laptop or desktop computers, video gaming devices and yes, even the old-fashioned television. They are a highly addictive substance that over time, engage your child's brain like no other activity and may make him or her crave to be on the device at the exclusion of all else.

You probably don't need me to tell you this. Just look around and you'll see kids (and adults too) walking while texting, or on social media. You'll see parks with kids sitting on benches playing video games instead of running around or swinging on the swings. Take two teen or pre-teen friends for a car ride and it's likely they'll text each other instead of hold an actual conversation or even look out the window. And video games? They have basically replaced any and all other form of card game, board game or physical game that we used to play pre-screens. Remember hop-scotch, jump rope and tag? Our kids don't know them.

If you are frustrated by all this, you're not alone. Parents everywhere ask me how to raise healthy and active children who read books in today's world where their attention, and ours, is constantly being grabbed by technology. This book is for them and for you. I believe we can live in a modern world, allowing technology's advances to improve our lives and make life easier while still ensuring that our children benefit from talking in-person, being physically fit, and my favorite, reading real books. In these pages, I'll show you how.

The Innovative Reading Method was created after two decades of my work in schools with children and parents, helping children become better readers and assisting parents in supporting their children as readers at home. Over time, it became increasingly clear that while parents wanted to help their children be better readers, they were up against a big problem: the ever-growing presence of screens both in and outside the home. My company, Innovative Reading, was born out of my passion to help parents manage screen time and increase their child's desire to read.

At first I was unsure how the message would be received. After all, technology is the wave of the future! However, the more I shared with parents my methods for managing screens, setting boundaries, and increasing children's reading time (and therefore lessening stress, as well as arguments over homework), the more parents wrote to me about their successes with my strategies.

Teachers and principals began writing too, and soon I was speaking at school district functions, teacher workshops and parent nights as well as at state and national conferences. This information was hitting home and needed to be shared!

Through my unique 5 step system found on the pages of this book, you too can be on the path to a happier home where mom and dad are on the same page about screen use, and the arguments with your child, pre-teen or teen are few and far between. Keep reading to get started managing screen time at home today, and let's help your child choose to read instead!

Who is this book for?

- Moms, dads and caregivers of kids ages 5-14 who live in the age of screens
- Parents who want to stop arguing with their child over screen time
- Parents who want to set boundaries around screen time with their child
- Parents who want to monitor their child's screen time for safety concerns
- Parents who wish their child would pick up a book instead of their phone and actually read it
- Parents who want to be on the same page with their spouse about screen use at home but find themselves arguing instead
- Moms and dads who feel guilty, unsure, anxious or unsettled around the amount of screen use either at home or in the world today and want a realistic, no-nonsense approach with practical strategies to make productive changes that everyone in the family can live with

Who am I and why should you listen to me?

I am a 20-year veteran educator in the New York State public school system. I have been a teacher, principal, director of curriculum and instruction, and assistant superintendent of schools. I have written countless articles on literacy, given dozens of workshops and talks on reading for both teachers and parents, and have been interviewed on podcasts and syndicated radio shows nationwide to share my message about the importance of developing a love of reading in children (and how to do it). In 2014 I won the prestigious Emerging Leaders Award by Phi Delta Kappa as one of the top 25 educators in the country for my groundbreaking work in literacy with middle and high school students. I have spoken on stages to thousands of parents just like you, helping them "get their child back" from the grip of screens and turn them on to healthier activities, such as reading. I invented The Innovative Reading Method and my 5 step program, Hooked on Screens, to give parents around the world the tools they need to end the battle of screen time at home and help their child love to read.

Are you ready to find out how you can stop the battle in your home? Let's go!

Lori and Greg's Story - Alexandria, VA

David is our 12-year-old son. He's been playing Xbox games religiously since his grandparents bought him the present for his birthday four years ago. At first they thought, and we agreed, it would be fun for him to play when he had friends over, after all, isn't this what kids do today?

We quickly noticed that David liked playing video games a lot. In a short period of time he went from a well-rounded kid who enjoyed shooting hoops in our driveway and going to the driving range with his father on Saturdays, to shutting himself up in the basement to play video games alone, even on sunny days.

We noticed other concerning behaviors as well. David became withdrawn. He had less friends over - except to play video games - and accepted fewer invitations to go places with other kids. He barely did his homework anymore, and only when we asked him repeatedly, which made him really agitated. In fact, he got agitated often.

My husband and I found ourselves constantly asking him to put the games down and do something else. Whether it was to clean his room, do his homework, sit down for dinner, go play outside, read a book or do just about anything else, we were always begging him to get off the Xbox.

David's behavior caused arguments between my husband and me. Even though we knew he shouldn't be playing video games constantly, we disagreed about how much is too much, and what we should do about it. Our arguing seemed to cause David to withdraw even further.

Asking doesn't work, yelling and threatening doesn't work, so what can we do? We need to do something!

Lori and Greg wrote me this letter in despair when they felt there was little hope. Does their story sound familiar to you at all? Or are you worried that this could happen to your child if you don't do something about it soon? There is good news. I worked with Lori and Greg and after a few short months on my program, they turned David's gaming habits around. Now he is a much healthier and happier child, and the family is under a lot less stress. Want to know the key to their success? Read on!

Chapter 1

Step 1 - Stop Nagging, Start Modeling

There are many little ways to enlarge your child's world.
Love of books is the best of all.

Jacqueline Kennedy Onassis

Dr. Carroll has been our saving grace. When we thought we had lost our son to the incredible pull of video games, we found her 5 step program and our home has been a much more peaceful place since implementing her strategies! We got our son back. Mike and Ella B. Alexandria, Va.

Problem:

Your child is always on a screen of some sort and you never talk to each other anymore. Whether it be Snapchat, Minecraft, Instagram, World of Warcraft or some other attention grabber (and keeper), your child puts a lot of time and energy on that and very little on healthy pursuits, like sports or reading. Plus, you find yourself doing a lot of yelling, nagging, bribing or pleading him to put the device down. How's that working for you? Not so well I bet. But what else can you do when he just won't listen?

What this step is about:

Parents need and want to stop nagging and begging their children to get off screens. Though it sometimes feels like the only recourse, it is not helping the situation and is actually putting your child in control. In this step, we quit these stressful actions and take back parental control by modeling positive behaviors of what we want our kids to be doing instead.

Benefit:

Parents gain back their sanity and stress diminishes. Nagging, yelling and begging your child to put down the screens are enormous stressors for you, your child, and any other family member within earshot. In this step, you will stop doing that and instead learn to use modeling techniques for the desired behaviors in order to decrease stress and bickering, and use your parental influence to coax the wanted behaviors out of your child.

How to do it:

I'm probably starting with the hardest piece of advice I have, and I know it's going to get tomatoes thrown at me. The truth is, however, that kids watch everything we do as adults (yes, everything!) and they are highly likely to repeat our behaviors, even when we tell them not to. In addition, have you ever noticed that nagging doesn't seem to be getting you anywhere long-term? You are probably nagging and yelling every single night, and even if you finally get the desired outcome, it doesn't last to the following day. For this reason, the first step to gaining control over screen time at home is to *stop* nagging your child to get off the screens. Sounds counterintuitive, I know, but hear me out.

I am not saying that you should stop talking with your child about screen use. You will talk to your child a lot about screens – in another step – but for now, I want you to stop *nagging* about them. That includes anything that looks or sounds like yelling, begging, pleading, growling, bribing or repeating that he needs to PUT.THAT.THING.DOWN.NOW!

Kids hate hearing you nag at them as much as you hate doing the nagging. Usually, I'm sure you've noticed, it doesn't work. Sure, sometimes it works temporarily, for a short period of time, after you've had to threaten to take away the cell phone for a month. But it doesn't *really* work. What you actually want is for your child to comply the first time you make the request, without having to resort to yelling or begging or threatening, and without having to ask over and over again.

Why doesn't nagging, yelling or begging work? Quite simply, you are giving your child a form of attention with these behaviors – and attention is what she craves from you. Even though this type of attention is not positive for either of you, and even though your child doesn't like to be nagged, it's still attention. Many kids will do what they need to do in order to get your undivided attention, even if it's the negative kind. When you nag or yell at your child to put away the screens and she doesn't comply, she knows that she'll get more attention from you and the form is predictable. Don't you want to break that pattern?

The first step on the way to end this negative attention-seeking-and-giving cycle is to stop the predictable action as a parent. When you no longer nag, yell, bribe or threaten to put down the screens, you'll really have your child wondering what is going on! Now you will truly have her attention (at least a small piece of it), instead of feeling ignored. This is good for both of you. Really good! And it's beneficial for everyone else in the household too. Siblings and spouses will certainly notice. Everyone will feel a lot calmer and that is the place we want to move forward from.

I know you are wondering how are you going to get your child off the cell phone if you don't ask her 100 times. We'll get there. For now, let's make a solid effort to stop nagging her to put it down. I promise, you'll thank me later!

Parent story: *I used to tell Sarah to put down her phone over and over and over again when it was time for dinner. No matter what I said or did, I could not get her to break away from it. Finally, after yelling upstairs about 10 times every evening, Sarah would come down to* *dinner and the meal was usually cold. Her younger sister was upset, my husband was frustrated and I was angry with her and myself for not knowing another way to handle it. All I wanted was a decent meal with my family, but getting my 12-year-old daughter to stop texting and sit down with us seemed nearly impossible, and she wasn't even a teenager yet. So when I heard Dr. Carroll tell the audience of parents to actually stop yelling and repeating to our kids to get off the phone, I thought, "There is no way that is going to work. Sarah will never come downstairs then!" I am pleased to say that I gave her method a try anyway since I had nothing to lose. Of course, I had to work the rest of the steps too but once I stopped the nagging, I felt like I gained back control. Now our dinners are peaceful.*

*Get my free download: **15 Phrases to Say to Your Child to Get Him to Read Without Threatening, Nagging or Yelling!** http://bit.ly/nonagging*

Parent As Role Model

Your child is still exhibiting the undesired behavior - constantly on a device - and you have agreed to stop asking him to get off it for the time being.

So now what? How is this going to get your child to put down the screen and start reading a book?

Your actions will speak louder than your words. I'm about to ask you to start modeling the behavior you want to see in your child.

I know, I know. You don't have time to read a book. In the evenings, you barely have time to cook dinner, make lunches and get everyone organized for the following morning before you fall into bed dead tired and have to do it all over again the next day. Many of you work a full-time job and then shuttle kids around to after-school programs and doctors' appointments. On the weekends, there's soccer and dance practice, birthday parties, church, housekeeping chores and a whole list of other commitments that you barely have time to breathe let alone read!

Does life feel like it's rushing past you and every day goes whizzing by? Do you feel like you NEVER have a spare minute to yourself with all the stuff that has to get done?

I get it, I do. We live in a world of modern conveniences that are supposed to make our lives easier and give us more time to spend with our family but somehow it doesn't seem to work like that.

Remember I said that your child wants your attention and when they want it bad enough, even nagging and yelling will be an acceptable form of it? Well, I mean it. I also promised that your child will NOTICE that you are no longer asking him to put down the screens. I am asking you to read now, just a few minutes every day in front of your child because your child is going to notice that too.

Also remember, whatever you do, your child is watching you. They watch the good behaviors, like telling them you love them, making the family healthy meals (ok, most of the time!), and helping an elderly neighbor with the groceries. They also watch the not-so-good behaviors, such as – well we all can come up with a few of those! (Achem, like binge watching crazy cat videos on Facebook instead of going to sleep…)

It follows then that the behaviors you are modeling are critical to pay attention to and adjust if you think they are not exactly what you want your child to do. Kids are way too smart to follow the, "Do as I say, not as I do" rule of yesteryear. They will do what you do, and then some, so be sure what you do is good modeling!

Not to get all social-sciencey here, but scientists have proof after years of studies that, "The apple doesn't fall far from the tree." You know this already: Children who grow up with parents who smoke tend to be smokers, children who grow up in homes with an alcoholic parent tend to abuse alcohol, and parents with low self-esteem tend to raise children with low self-esteem. Over and over again it proves to be true with the good, the bad and the ugly: teen moms raise children more likely to be teen moms, homes with domestic violence tend to raise aggressive kids, families whose parents went to college have kids who go to college and families who eat healthy foods tend to raise children who choose to eat healthy foods.

And yes, parents who put down the screens and pick up a book tend to raise children who choose to read.

What am I saying here, exactly?

Put down your phone and pick up a book in front of your child. Do it for 10 minutes a night. (More is better!) Yes, really.

Don't think your own smartphone use is actually a problem? Maybe it isn't. But let's take an honest look.

Action Step:

For the next 3 days, whenever you are home and your kids are in sight, count how many times you check your phone (or other tech device, like a tablet, everything counts). Record this number. Extra points if you keep track of how long you were on it each time.

Tally - How many times did you:
Send a text?
Check email?
Watch a YouTube video?
Engage on Facebook?
Check out Instagram or Pinterest?
Read an online blog post/article?
Open an app?
Do any other activity on a screen? (Answering a phone call doesn't count.)

According to recent studies, if you are like most adults, you are checking your phone on average 110 times over the course of a day (other studies show it's closer to 150)! Countless minutes get easily eaten by sending a "quick text" or email, or opening Facebook and before you know it, getting absorbed in Dodo videos. Do this daily with your kids around and you've just modeled lots of screen activity for your child.

Could any of that time, even just a few minutes, have been spent reading a book (or magazine or newspaper article)?

Maybe the bandwidth it takes to read an actual book is larger than you can expend right now. I get that too. Believe me, there are many days (even most days) I feel the same way; my brain is just too fried to follow a story, or the advice of a self-help book. So in honor of all those times, refer to my **Resources** section for some quality suggestions of short stories, short advice or just plain old short sentences.

This step has two parts and on the surface they seem relatively easy to do (once you find a few minutes to squeeze reading into each day). However, I realize that I am asking you to change routine actions and that can be a tough challenge! Know that we are not aiming for perfection here. We are going for "good enough". We are striving for enough actions that your child sits up and takes notice that there are changes going on around here. So spend several days on this step until you get it down before you move on. Get comfortable with not nagging or yelling about screens for a few days while you do what you can to put reading materials in your hands in front of your kids. (Read at the stove while stirring the pasta if you must.) Watch what happens to your kids, and even your spouse if you choose not to tell him what's going on just yet. I bet you'll have a good giggle at their reactions…

This does not mean that we won't talk to our family members about screen time and also about reading. We definitely will! However, it is my strong philosophy that we should be the change first and to do that well, we must begin looking within ourselves at what we need to do differently so that others can be a reflection of our best actions.

Vera's Story - Tampa, FL

I was irritated at first when Dr. Carroll told me I had to put down my phone if I wanted my daughters to put down theirs. After all, I use my phone for work, even when I'm home, and I needed to answer emails off-hours. I just didn't see it as the same as my girls constantly checking social media. I knew I had to get control of the situation, however, as my 11 and 13-year-olds were totally obsessed. So I took her advice and tried to put the phone down in front of my kids for 3 days. IT WAS HARD! I mean, really hard. Like, nearly impossible. It was then that I realized that I was addicted too. Wow.

I had some soul searching to do, and I was only on the first step! I began to understand that I was making excuses for myself to be on a screen constantly but not allowing my daughters the same privilege. Checking social media is as important to them as my work emails are to me. I knew we had to talk and I had to own up to my behaviors. I also acknowledged I could batch-answer my work emails at points during the day. The truth was, I didn't need to be on my phone constantly.

I decided I'd try to read in front of my kids. To be honest, I didn't really like to read. But Dr. Carroll made it easier for me by sharing lots of resources that I could like, even actually find interesting, that weren't boring fiction novels. Once I started reading in front of my girls, I felt proud of myself for being the reader I wanted them to be. It was so much easier to talk to them about getting off their cell phones when I began modeling what I wanted them to do. It seems so obvious now but frankly I just didn't see it before.

Final takeaway:

Nagging, yelling or threatening your child to put down the screens doesn't work long-term and makes everyone feel bad. By modeling reading instead, you will feel good about your actions and your child will too. Commit today to taking Step 1 and follow the rest of the steps in this book.

Read books and other printed materials (such as magazines and newspapers) in front of your child as often as you can (at least 10 minutes a day) if you want him to put down the screens and spend time reading.

Questions parents ask:

"If I am reading an article on my phone or on a tablet, does that count as modeling reading?"

My answer is no. When you are on a device, your child doesn't know if you are reading an article or checking Facebook. She can't tell when you are looking at a screen if you are reading a book that you downloaded or looking at Instagram unless she is standing over your shoulder, which most of the time she is not. All screens (including ereaders like Nook and Kindle) look like they are being used for purposes other than reading, even when we are truly reading. It's for that reason that I say you must read a paper book (or a paper magazine or newspaper) if you want to truly model reading in front of your child. Eventually, when your child is consistently reading independently, you can go back to the ereader again if you choose. Or, you may certainly use it when you read without your child present.

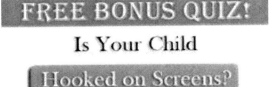

FREE BONUS QUIZ!
Is Your Child
Hooked on Screens?
http://bit.ly/screentimequiz

Chapter 2

Step 2 -Tap Into Your Child's Interests

*There are perhaps no days of our childhood we lived
so fully as those spent with a favorite book.*

Marcel Proust

If you have a garden and a library, you have everything you need.

Marcus Tullius Cicero

Until I did Step 2, I didn't really know what my child was interested in besides screens. Truthfully, I don't think my child knew either, because in our home we didn't focus on interests. Now we do and he's learning what he likes that has nothing to do with video games. Looking back, he seemed depressed before but I didn't even recognize it.
Bob H. Wichita, KS

Problem: Your child doesn't read because he says it's boring. He stopped picking up books years ago and now only reaches for video games. He clearly finds those interesting! Aside from gaming, you're not sure what interests him anymore, because the more he plays video games, the less he does anything else. You wish he'd stop gaming and go outside, pursue a hobby or pick up a book and actually read it. When you tell him to stop playing video games, it starts a big fight. He says you just don't understand him.

What this step is about: Kids who have interests aside from screens are healthier, happier kids. Period. When kids have interests, they are less likely to be drawn to screens because there are other activities they like and want to do. In this step, we work to ensure your child develops interests outside of video games and social media and that you as a parent know what those interests are.

Benefit: You can begin to coax your child away from screens to pursue healthier options. Plus, what we are interested in we want to learn more about. How do we learn? Reading is one great way to gain information.

How to do it:

Why are kids on screens all the time? Well, there are many reasons, from the simple fact that kids find the content relevant and interesting, to the darker, more sinister side of technology. This includes the creators of social media and gaming content lacing the web and games with addictive images and strategies to purposefully hook young and old minds alike. (Yes, that's really true.) This keeps them wanting to continuously engage with the game or website - such as social media sites - and not with real life. In addition, video games and social media provide countless hours of feel-good instant gratification without having to do much for it in return. The human mind seriously loves this one-sided, convenient form of lazy entertainment.

This is a huge problem, and when you start to understand that screen addiction is real and that it isn't your fault or your child's, it may make you sad, even angry. You are fighting a bigger battle than you may have known before. We all are.

You are not alone. Every child and every parent in the modern world is fighting this same battle. Some families find it harder than others, and part of that is because some brains find gaming, social media and internet use more addictive than others. Just like with drugs, alcohol and smoking. Some people find these substances way more appealing, and harder to give up, than others do.

It seems, however, that every child on some level has an interest in screens. At least this is what I hear from parents and teachers at all the conferences, workshops and summits where I give talks. Therefore, no matter if you'd say your child is "addicted" today or not, I suggest you still follow along with what we are doing here. An ounce of prevention…

In Step 2, you keep doing what you have learned in Step 1. It's important that you continue to model reading for your child every day for 10 minutes (or come close, remember we're not going for perfection). In Step 1 I also asked you to stop doing any action that resembled nagging, yelling, begging, bribing or threatening your child to put down the screens and we covered why this wasn't a good strategy to use for long-term results. Hopefully you have given this a try and are feeling a bit calmer (though your child may still be on screens more than you like). If you haven't given Step 1 a try, it's important that you do that before moving on to Step 2. This program builds, one step upon the next. It's not possible to be successful with the next step until you have implemented the step before it.

Again, *we are not going for perfection*. We are going for "good enough". Once you feel you are mostly not nagging and you're reading in front of your child for about 10 minutes most days of the week, then you are ready for Step 2. You can always improve each step along the way – with practice, you will do just that.

In Step 2, our goal is to define what healthy activities interest your child so you can help him focus on the interest through the activity itself as well as read about it, and lessen the use of screens.

Everyone on the planet has likes and dislikes. Everyone is motivated to move towards pleasure and away from pain. We all want to pursue what makes us happy and fulfilled, while avoiding anything that doesn't create those emotions. Therefore, everyone, including the youngest children, have interests (even though some might not be developed yet).

Interests are the activities, subjects and ideas that invite our pursuit. They can be a sport, a hobby, or an item that we want to engage in.

They get us excited to wake up each day. Depending on what they are, they may be easy to access - like baking cookies, or harder to access, such as downhill skiing or fly fishing. They may be an inexpensive hobby, like rock collecting or bird watching, or costlier both in terms of time and money – hello golf!

Many children have lots of interests, some have a few and some seemingly have none. If you feel your child is in the latter category, check out the **Questions parents ask** section at the end of this chapter for guidance on what you can do.

With schedules so busy today, many kids and adults don't have as much time as they'd like to pursue their interests. I know you know how that feels! I bet there are many hobbies, sports or activities you'd just LOVE to do if only there was more time. I hear you.

Personally, I'd love to have more time to make quilts. I am so passionate about fabric, sewing, and putting all the pieces together to create beautiful hand-made objects that can be treasured for years to come. I'd love to spend days on end sewing, but because of the length of time it takes to make a quilt as well as the amount of space a true sewing room takes up, I am just not able to do it right now.

So, do I squelch this passion completely? No. In order to satisfy my quilting itch I do the next best thing. I read about it - a lot!

I get several quilting magazines delivered to my house each month and I thoroughly enjoy pouring over each one, dreaming about the patterns I'll choose next time I have a stretch of days off. I read books on it too, about top quilters and their creations, the stories behind the quilts or the history of certain styles and trends. I even read how-to sections for when I am going to need it, such as how to attach a binding or how to do paper piecing.

While I am not actually quilting, I am scratching that itch, for the time being, and getting a lot of reading in as well.

So what does this have to do with you and your child? My example is to show you that what we find interesting, we want to know more about. If our passion is great enough, we'll want to learn all we can about the topic. It's just human nature to pursue what makes us happy. To learn more about a topic, we can do one of a few things. We can watch videos on it (YouTube has endless hours on any topic you want), we can talk to others who are already experts, or we can read about it.

Our goal in this step is to get your child to want to read about what she is interested in, and then pursue the one interest she is most excited about.

Action step:

Take a few moments to answer the following questions. Take your time and really think about each one. Be open and honest with yourself, no one else will see this but you. If you have more than one child, do this for each.

- List the top 5 interests your child appears to have.
- Of these, which are healthy pursuits that you would want to support him to be further involved in? For example, we are trying to limit screen time so playing video games and Snapchatting with friends don't make this list. Playing a musical instrument, playing a sport or raising animals, for example, do.
- Answer these questions for each item above that makes the cut.
- How do you know your child has this interest?
- What are the signs, behaviors, emotional responses and words he uses when pursuing this interest? For example, does his face light up? Does she get very talkative? Does he tune out the rest of the world when engaged in this activity?
- How does your child already pursue this interest? List the activities he is currently doing that align with this interest.
- What else could your child be doing to increase his engagement with this interest?

- As a parent, are you able to support this interest? Is it doable for you (in terms of time, money, etc)?

- Where can reading be incorporated into this interest to increase his engagement? Which single interest would be a good topic to read about in order to increase your child's motivation to learn more about it and gain new skills?

- **Bonus question:** How is the use of screens interfering with the pursuit of this interest for your child? In other words, if screen-time were minimized, how else might your child be pursuing this interest?

*Note: There is an important distinction between interests and passions. They are not the same thing. Passions are much stronger than interests. Although we'd love our child to be passionate about an activity, hobby or sport, the truth is many children have not developed their skill set or knowledge base about the hobby, sport or other pursuit enough to call it a true passion yet. This is just fine – for the sake of this work, any interest that your child shows an inkling to pursue can be effective. Over time, as his skills and knowledge about this topic grow, a passion may easily develop, keeping him hooked on a wholesome activity, possibly for years to come.

Next steps:

The questions above should help define your child's interests and give you an idea of which one would be good to pursue through reading.

In Step 3 we are going to discuss how to move your child off screens and into books by using interests, so be sure you complete this step before moving forward. If you don't know what interest would motivate your child, read the **Questions parents ask** section below for ideas.

Marlo and Celine's Story - Austin, TX

Caleb was involved in lots of activities when he was younger, but he never really seemed to gravitate to any one thing much, and as parents, we didn't push it. Now we also see that meant we didn't help him pursue anything in-depth, and that led to him quitting just about every activity he tried as he became a 'tween. Of course, technology was an interest to him, and he spent plenty of time on screens. We assumed that was ok and what all kids were doing, but it seemed to get worse over time to the point where he was becoming withdrawn and isolated. It was even difficult to get him out of his room for meals. That's when my wife and I began to worry about him.

We realize now that helping develop his interests from a young age may have curbed some of his desire for screen time. We were encouraged to hear that it's 'never too late' from Dr. Carroll, and so when Caleb was in 7th grade we started making several changes according to her program. We began to model reading as well as some of our own interests, and worked to include Caleb in them whenever we could. Of course, in the beginning he balked, but we didn't quit.

One thing Caleb always seemed to like was animals. He had wanted a dog since he was young but we didn't think we had the time for it. Now we had to rethink that decision. Could Caleb take an interest in a pet? We took Dr. Carroll's advice for children to volunteer and we talked him into spending the afternoon helping out at a dog shelter. We offered to bring home a dog if he put forth solid effort that day and there was a good fit for a pet. Finally, we saw Caleb's eyes light up again for the first time in years!

That day, Caleb worked hard with other volunteers to walk and wash dogs, feed them and do basic grooming. He felt so good about himself, he couldn't wait to go back the following weekend – his idea! We also brought home an adorable mixed breed puppy that Caleb absolutely loves and takes care of himself. He's now reading about dog training from some books we got at the library.

Our son is still interested in gaming, but he spends much more time off video games now enjoying life and his new commitment to the shelter and his own dog. We no longer worry that all he does is play video games. We can't thank Dr. Carroll enough for her sound advice!

Final takeaway:

Every child has interests, even if they don't know it. It is up to the parents to expose those interests and then help your child pursue them. The more you support her interests, the less time she will have for screens. The more you encourage reading about the interest, the more she will want to learn about it through research.

Questions parents ask:
What if my child doesn't seem to have any interests?

Some children, especially during the pre-teen and teen years, appear to have no interests outside of their friends, social media and video games. While this behavior is not all that uncommon, it also isn't healthy, so you want to make an effort to develop other wholesome life-time pursuits. It's a good idea to begin to help children develop interests when they are young, as they are more impressionable by you and they haven't entered the years where peers have a strong influence on them. However, it is never too late to start and often older children just need guidance and a firm push toward an activity they will come to enjoy.

How do I spark a new interest in my child?

Parents can model their own interests for their child by participating in clubs and groups or engaging in an interest right at home, even in the little time you have. If it's appropriate to bring your child with you to a meeting or event, do so to expose your child to your activities and gauge if they have any motivation to see more.

You can also talk to your child about just trying one session of a class or lesson to see if they want to continue. Many dance classes, martial arts studios, painting classes and music studios will offer the first session at a low price or even free to see if your child will like it. Try a few and see what seems to stick.

Make a bargain with your child. It's not OK to sit home and do nothing (aka text friends, hang out on Instagram or play Minecraft for hours). Give your child options for participating in a healthy activity of their choice and sign him up for lessons, clubs or events. Don't offer screen time as the reward, however. If you need a bargaining chip, perhaps he can get out of a chore one time instead, or stay up an hour later on the weekend to play a board game with the family.

How do I ensure my child develops interests as she grows up?

Getting children involved in activities from their youngest years will set them up for a life of various interests. Children should have responsibilities around the home, and there should be expectations that they are active in some sort of physical exercise as well as opportunities to help others. These three expectations help set the stage for an active, engaged, motivated child who feels a sense of commitment to their home, to themselves and to others. From here, dozens of various interests will inevitably develop.

Examples:

Responsibilities at home: dishwashing after meals, cleaning his room, doing the laundry, caring for the family pet, helping a parent wash the family car, make her own lunch or cook dinner (with or without parent assistance)

Physical exercise: Join a recreational sports team, take dance lessons, do yoga with a parent, take a martial art, shoot hoops, take family hikes on weekends

Help others: volunteer at a community-based garden or tag sale, donate food to a soup kitchen or food drive, read to dogs or cats at an animal shelter, join a youth organization or church group with a mission, volunteer to help an elderly neighbor once a week

FREE BONUS QUIZ!

Is Your Child

Hooked on Screens?

http://bit.ly/screentimequiz

Visit www.InnovativeReading.com for free resources!

Chapter 3

Step 3 - Create a Reader-Friendly Home™

So please, oh PLEASE, we beg, we pray, go throw your TV set away. And in its place you can install, a lovely bookshelf on the wall.

Roald Dahl

When we counted up the screens in our house we were shocked at how many we had. With three kids and two adults, every room had multiple electronic devices and it never occurred to us this was a problem, until we couldn't get our kids off of them. With Dr. Carroll's help we replaced much of their screen time with reading time. Our kids are emotionally happier for it, and we all love the reading nooks we created in the process! Marla and Tony P. Jacksonville, FL.

Problem:

You have a home full of the latest technology gadgets. Smartphones, TVs, tablets and computers can be found in every room in the house. We like the look of these shiny screens, while docking stations, charging stands and cradles keep them neatly at bay.

However, where are all the books?
What books am I talking about?
Exactly.

What this step is about:

It's time to take a good look around your home and ask yourself what is being promoted without saying a word. Is it screens, or is it books? We'll look at how to minimize the presence of screens and maximize reading materials so the home can help you promote books without even talking about it.

Benefit:

Our home environment has a strong influence on our minds, and says a lot about what we value. If it is bright, cheerful and organized, we are more likely to be positive, happy and calm. If it is dark, dreary or cluttered, it is possible we will be sad, depressed or anxious. Likewise, an environment that promotes books and minimizes screens shows kids that reading is valued here over video games and social media, and that is the message we want to be sending!

How to do it:

Look around your home and count how many digital devices you see. If you count between 10-14, you would be like the average household in the modern era. Most homes today with two adults and a few kids have several televisions, cell phones, and tablets, as well as multiple laptop and desktop computers. You may even have separate video game consoles, MP3 players, ereaders, and more. The average family keeps several devices in each room, on full display, with charging cables at the ready on counter tops and desks to be able to power up at a moment's notice. Technology at our fingertips has become something we can't live without, even in the bathroom. (Admit it, you've used your cell phone in there, haven't you?)

While there is nothing inherently wrong with the convenience of having screens around the house, the problem is we are making access to them, all the time, a bit *too* convenient. If there's a TV in every room, chances are we'll turn it on when we are cooking dinner, sitting in the living room, or laying in bed. Likewise, if our cell phones are in every room with us – since they're like an appendage – we (kids *and* adults) will use them all the time. Am I right?

In Step 3, I am encouraging you to create a Reader-Friendly Home™. This means that books need to take a front seat in the home, and technology needs to take a step back. Even a small step back would be beneficial to make room for reading in your family's life.

Remember in Step 1 how we talked about you modeling reading for your child? Well Step 3 builds on that with your home. We are going to create a living space that models reading for your child as well – by displaying books, magazines and other reading materials out for easy pickins. We'll also ensure we have places to sit that invite reading, thinking and dreaming (that don't have a charging station nearby). The goal here is to make reading the easy choice, and screens a harder choice, at least some of the time. To do so we need to make reading enticing, fun, relaxing and something to look forward to. We need to remove any stigma it may have with your child about being boring, difficult, hard to access, or akin to work. In the upcoming pages, I'll show you how.

Now look around your home again. In how many places do you see reading materials? Where are the books, magazines, and newspapers? Are there bookcases in places where the family gathers, and in the children's bedrooms? Are there places that are inviting for children to read, with comfortable seating and good lighting?

These are the things that make a home reader-friendly, and we're going to start shifting your home in this direction so that there are lots of appealing spaces for children to read. At the same time we're going to make technology a wee bit harder to access so it isn't the very first thing your kids can reach.

Think of it like food in the kitchen. If you keep a plate of cookies on the counter, how easy is it for the kids (and you!) to grab one every time they pass by? If you put a bag of whole carrots next to the cookies, even still, which one is everyone going to grab? I know I'm going for the cookies every time! But, if instead you put baby carrots in an attractive bowl, add a yummy dip, and hide the cookies away on a top shelf in the cabinet, the family will most likely eat some carrots, with dip, and even pull up a stool for a moment and have another. See where I'm going with this analogy?

Action steps:

Let's make this easy and start with establishing one cozy reading nook. I'll keep it simple and use bullets here. Check off as many as you can to create this space:

- Ensure there is at least one cozy chair/bean bag/inviting rug with pillows and a throw or afghan in the home where your child feels comfortable hanging out.

- Add plenty of quality lighting so the eyes don't have to work too hard.

- Keep a basket/shelf/box of books, magazines, comics, graphic novels, travel pamphlets and other reading material readily accessible; rotate the options regularly (but keep the favorites).

- Keep the noise level in the reading area minimal, or create a noise-free time when your child can read and relax without distractions.

- Show you value words; decorate the walls with words and letters in the form of posters, wall hangings, block letters, wall stickers, decals and artwork; try words on bedspreads, area rugs, curtains, throws and pillows; add a box of magnetic poetry with a magnet board.

- Have your child help create the reading nook, and add his own personal touches like book choices, his artwork, and items he built or enjoys - if he creates the space, he's much more likely to use it!

Once you have created one space for your kids, branch out. Where else around the house can you add better reading light? A basket of books and magazines? Words on the wall? If you need some inspiration -

this would be a quality use of a few minutes on Pinterest. Just search 'reading nooks'. Be sure to get in and get out and spend the bulk of your time decorating, then reading!

Fast fact:

Most kids like reading at least one genre or style of book (even if they say they hate to read). Find out what that style is and stock the bookshelves you put in his room. (There is at least one bookshelf or book basket in there, right?) Not sure yet what that style is? Try comics, graphic novels or any book with humor. In survey after survey of children who say they don't like to read, they usually say they will read if it's funny.

Now let's talk about what needs to go. Do your best here, this is not going to be easy, especially if everyone has gotten used to these little luxuries. Be firm, and don't let a little whining from your kids (or spouse) deter you from making a major impact. Remember, we are not striving for perfection, so even accomplishing just one action on this list will be a solid step in the right direction.

- No TV in your child's bedroom, and younger children should not have computers in their bedrooms either. (No wiggle room here!)

- Make it difficult to access the diversions like video games by putting them away after use. Put tablets in drawers and laptops in their sleeves - they're better protected and collect less dust like that anyway.

- Pass the basket at dinner time – the cell phone basket that is! No cell phones at the table (no TV either) means you will actually talk, and listen, to each other. This is a great time to talk about what everyone is reading lately. Bring out an interesting magazine article to discuss.

- Don't buy screens you don't "need", and young children should **not** get cell phones. Did you know that Bill Gates, Steve Jobs and many others in the technology field didn't allow their own children to have smartphones until age 14 (or older)? Considering they're the experts, there must be good reasons why!

- Save the special movies and video games for long car trips and other times you really need to keep kids busy. Expect that kids will make better choices in their usual free time like playing outside, reading a book, playing board games, doing a puzzle, or creating artwork or crafts.

- Stop cleaning up the reading materials all the time. It's true, screens have a neat appearance and books, magazines and newspapers are a bit messy looking, but for the sake of modeling, leave the reading stuff out! We want kids to see what we are reading, that books and magazines are so awesome we leave them out, and that spontaneous reading happens in this home.

- Create a "screen-use" contract with your family (include your spouse) that describes when and where screen use is acceptable and when and where it is not. Let everyone participate and have a voice. Then hold each other accountable and be sure there are fair and meaningful repercussions for those that break the pact.

A home that's reader-friendly has lots of child-appropriate reading materials to choose from. This is critical! You can set up the space with a cozy chair, good lighting, several pillows and even decree that it stays tech-free but if there aren't loads of great books, magazines and articles to choose from, reading is not going to happen. We need your child to want to be in this space, *and* choose to read when she goes there.

This is where Step 2 becomes super useful. You have done the work it takes to find out your child's interests and what she gets enthused about. If your child didn't have any deep interests, you've begun to try to establish at least one by introducing her to options and seeing what sticks.

Now we want to use those interests, (even if they are just budding) to hook kids to books. If we can relate reading to fun activities, children will begin to think that reading can be fun. The problem is that many kids who say they "hate to read" find it boring because they are not reading about what they find interesting.

Don't we all get bored reading what we don't find interesting? I definitely do!

Therefore, in Step 3, it's critical to load up the cozy reading nook, and other bookcases and baskets around the home, with reading materials that your child will love. They can be books, magazines, newspaper articles, pamphlets from places they love or want to visit (Disney!) and any other print resources you can collect.

Need some ideas to get the juices flowing? Ask your local librarian or book store clerk for recommendations of books and magazines that are suitable for your child's age group in the area of her interest. You'll be amazed at all the options there are that you didn't know existed! There are new books for children, pre-teen and teens written constantly, so you can tap into brand new titles as well as trusted treasures with just a little help from someone in-the-know. A quick search on websites like Amazon or Barnes and Noble can yield lots of good options as well. For universal success, graphic novels (not your comics of yesteryear!) work for most reluctant readers and just about every kid is tickled by books in the humor genre.

Kids love magazines, and who can blame them? I love them too. There are quick articles to read, they are written for high interest, with images, charts and graphs to help your child visualize and understand the text. Most magazines are written with a specific interest in mind, from sports, to science to horses and cheerleading, there is something for everyone. Subscribe to several magazines in your child's area of interest and keep that reading corner stocked!

Get my free download: **Dr. Carroll's List of Favorite High Interest Magazines for Ages 2-Teen!**

http://bit.ly/FavoriteMagazines

Mona's Story - Colorado Springs, CO

I didn't want to put the tech devices away. Frankly, it seemed like a lot of work and I liked having my iPad out in the kitchen so I could look up recipes and scroll through Facebook while I was cooking dinner each evening. The girls also had TVs in their rooms which they watched, mostly on weekends, but it kept them quiet and I was skeptical about removing them. Would it actually help anything? Would it cause more arguments? We were already fighting daily about too much screen time so we didn't need more to argue about. I decided to tackle the smaller items first and see how the new practices went with my family.

We began with a cell phone basket at meals because having at least a few meals a week where we actually talked to each other was important to me. I already harped on the kids about not bringing their cell phones to the table so this was not going to be a shocker to them, or my husband. What I liked about the cell phone basket was that it stopped any sneaking a text here and there under the table or a "bathroom break" which was actually a text break in the middle of the meal. Plus, the adults put their cell phones in too, which stopped my husband from checking his emails at dinner, "just once" and frankly gave me no excuses either. We all agreed we could survive the 30 – 40 minutes it took to serve and eat dinner. Now we have distraction-less meals again. I love this!

I then decided to keep the screens I had in the kitchen in a drawer unless I was using them, instead of leaving them out on the countertop. That meant my iPad and cell phone went in a drawer much of the time. I noticed this stopped me from mindlessly checking Facebook several times an evening, which was a welcomed break I didn't know I needed. It also caused me to take out my old cookbooks again; I forgot I even had some of them! I still use a few favorite apps for recipes, but I decided that reading cookbooks was modeling reading for my kids, so I like that I can multi-task that!

One weekend, my girls and I created a reading nook for each of them. We had a loft area at the top of the staircase that was unused and the perfect place to toss a couple of bean bag chairs, pillows and a bookcase. They wanted to hang some artwork from school which helped make it their own. Next, we collected books from around the house and added some more from the public library to give the girls lots of choices. I wondered if they would choose to use this area to read. At first they were hanging out there on their cell phones so we had a conversation about the reading part! We added a cell phone basket on the table around the corner and gave the girls a challenge to leave phones there for 20 minutes while reading in the nook. I can see it's a struggle for them to not check their cell phones constantly, but they're trying. And I am seeing them go to this nook and pick up a book or a magazine a few times a week now. Before they had this space, I never saw them do that!

Since the other ideas worked so well, I think I may tackle the TVs in the bedrooms after all.

We are so grateful to Dr. Carroll for her ideas. They have truly helped our family. It was amazing to start seeing progress with our daughters right away and now we feel empowered to continue this path.

Final takeaway:

Just like you, your home can model too. When the books are prominent and technology takes a back seat, children are more likely to choose books. Creating a reading nook all their own helps children feel the invitation to read even more.

Questions parents ask:
How many books are needed to create a reading nook?

It's about the quality of choices rather than the quantity of materials. If a reading nook is filled with books that your child doesn't like, it's not going to be useful in getting her to want to read. Choose a few books and a few magazines, rotate them monthly and get your child involved in creating a cozy and welcoming space.

I don't like to look at books and magazines, I find them messy. How can I do this?

Fill a decorative basket that can be tucked under a chair or end table to keep the books in one neat spot. Use a quiet corner that is not a high traffic area for the cozy reading space and install a small bookshelf to store the reading materials. To satisfy the craving to be organized, give your child the task to arrange them by height or color, or alphabetize by author. Enlist your child in keeping the area neat and toss old magazines and newspapers so they don't pile up (or cut them up to create a vision board, see Step 4).

My child wants to bring his tablet to the reading nook. What do I do?

Have a discussion with your child that this screen-free spot is for reading, writing in a journal and daydreaming only. Talk about why everyone needs a safe space like this and discuss candidly why electronic devices are not allowed. Enlist his help to decorate the space and decide what time he will spend there. Have him choose the reading resources and the basket or bookshelf, as well as any artwork or other décor he wants to add. When the space feels like his and he understands why the rules exist, he is much more likely to respect them. If the tablet is an ereader (like a Kindle or Nook), that can get tricky. Many of them can also be gaming devices and you don't want to have to police this spot. I suggest paper only here to keep it simple.

FREE BONUS QUIZ!

Is Your Child

Hooked on Screens?

http://bit.ly/screentimequiz

Visit www.InnovativeReading.com for free resources!

Chapter 4

Step 4 - Set Goals Through Journals and Vision Boards

Any book that helps a child to form a habit of reading, to make reading one of his deep and continuing needs, is good for him.

Maya Angelou

I was skeptical that my child would want to keep a journal before we talked about it. But once we got it going, I learned she loved to write in it and that led us to creating amazing vision boards together. I am glad I pushed past my doubts on this. Tisha has goals I never would have heard about! Renee B. New York, NY

Problem:

Do any of these resonate with you?

- Your child isn't enthusiastic about anything
- When you ask your child what he wants to do, or eat, or where he'd like to go, the answer is always a shoulder shrug and, "I dunno"
- He doesn't seem motivated to get up in the morning, even on a weekend
- Your child tells you often, "I'm bored"

- If you don't figure out an activity for your child to do, she will always pick up a screen and stay glued to it
- Your child seems listless, unfocused, lackadaisical or spiritless
- Your child turns to gaming, social media or YouTube videos for constant entertainment and personal gratification, but doesn't look forward to real-life events
- Your child has plenty of energy but he expends it only on video games

What this step is about:

Kids are natural dreamers when they are young, but as they get older, those dreams often fade away. However, research tells us that even adults who "dream" by setting goals and revisiting them often are much more likely to achieve their goals and have greater success and happiness in life than those who don't. We must teach children that it's important to not only dream, but to memorialize those dreams (aka goals) in either a journal, a vision board or both. This keeps them alive and real, and within reach.

Benefit:

Children who learn at an early age to think big and go-for-it gain confidence, learn how to tolerate risk and accept failure, and are more resilient. In my program, we also use this mindset to enhance your child's reading interest while minimizing their attraction to screens. A win-win-win!

How to do it:

You work hard to give your child a good life and all the things she needs. There is plenty of food, a good home, lots of clothes and she's involved in activities outside of school. Still, something seems off. You go through the motions of each day – your whole family does – but what are you really aiming at? What are your kids hoping for in the future? What are they dreaming about? What would they really like to be good, even amazing at?

Everyone needs to work towards goals in order to feel like their life has purpose. Many adults know this well, and they spend a lot of time both in their personal and professional lives setting goals and creating a vision about what they want their future to look like. Those who make the effort to plan and self-reflect in this way usually reap the benefits of an incredible life.

Some of us review our goals in our head, adding a new idea and taking out what doesn't serve us anymore. Others take it a step further and record these goals and dreams in a notebook, or journal, even rewriting them daily as a constant reminder. To confirm that large numbers of people are writing about their goals and dreams, check out the massive journal section of the next bookstore you visit. Or Google the words *goals journal, productivity tracker, planner* or other similar keywords to see the hundreds of options that come up to write and record your dreams in one place.

There are also dozens, if not hundreds of books and blogs on the topic of goal-setting and creating a vision for your future. There's a reason it's so popular. It *works* to create an amazing life you love.

Having a personal vision and setting goals serves us on many levels. Making time to think about our dreams, write them down and revisit them often is a gift to ourselves both now and in the future. It sets us up for success today and helps us know what next steps to take tomorrow. The endgame is our own design, and now we can create a road map to get there.

It also allows us to consider what is important in life, weed out what we don't want and get crystal clear on what we do want to bring more of into our world. It gives us the space to concentrate on our interests, to have a reason to get up in the morning, and to pursue what excites us. It helps us create meaning.

I write my goals down each morning when I get up. I keep a leather-bound journal at my desk and make a cup of tea. I rise at the wee hours of the morning to spend at least 20 minutes dreaming and goal setting for my near and distant future. I have been doing this for years, and I can't imagine a morning without it. I know others who have their own unique system, but the result is the same. A vision for the future is created, written down, revisited, and eventually either comes to fruition or morphs along the way as we learn and grow. Not every dream is perfectly realized, but the practice of envisioning what you want and how you'll get it ensures that you have a purpose for each and every day - to work on and fulfill that dream! It also makes crystal clear the time-wasters in life, the things we do that don't bring us closer to those goals and dreams.

Journaling goals is such an amazing practice, I've often wondered why we don't teach it to children in schools as a genre of writing. In my opinion as a lifelong educator, it should be a mandatory part of the curriculum. As a sixth grade teacher for seven years, I taught my students to keep a journal to record their thoughts, feelings, dreams and goals. When we wrote in this journal, I turned down the lights and played "thinking music" to relax and engage the mind. It quickly became each class's favorite part of the day. Years later, several of my students told me they still had that journal and described the dynamic impact it had on their lives.

Powerful stuff, right?

I believe children should journal their goals and dreams, and not wait until adulthood to take up this practice. It's just too important and beneficial to wait! However, for kids to make a habit of journaling, we need to teach them how and model the practice. It's hard for some kids to think about big goals and dreams, especially if it hasn't been discussed at home yet. It's harder still for many kids to write them down, particularly if they don't like writing.

Regardless of the challenges, I firmly believe that for all kids, having dreams and setting goals is a critical step in living a fulfilled life. A life where the everyday is enjoyed and savored, instead of the alternative realities that technology creates through video game fantasy lands and the unfulfilling, unrealistic, FOMO-inspired worlds of Instagram and Snapchat. Plus, setting goals leads to other healthier activities (like reading!) because to achieve most objectives in life, we need to learn new things. What is one of the best and easiest ways to learn? Read.

To that end, making an effort to help kids live for today while planning for and getting excited about their future is always time well spent, and the younger we get them started the better (though it is never too late to begin).

Oh, and one more thing. When kids are dreaming about their hopes and setting goals for themselves, they are stimulating a section of their brain that being on a screen will *never* touch. They are developing an intelligence that activates a part of their brain that is critical for future success. What happens to this part of the brain when too much time is spent on screens? It actually *erodes*. Yeah, not good.

Create the map with vision boards

While journaling is a beautiful practice, children tend to be visual learners (like most of us). We can read directions, but when we see a map, the path becomes much clearer. Photographs, drawings, images, charts, graphs and illustrations all help us visualize so that we can then put words to our thoughts. This is why many people who dream big and set goals create vision boards (even those who also journal). This is also why I now suggest in the path to journaling with kids, we start with creating a vision board.

What is a vision board? A vision board is any kind of display of images collected and curated by the goal-setter and organized in a pleasing way that represents what you want to have, do or be in life. This board can be hung on a wall, kept in a binder, used as a desk blotter or propped on a stand, as long as it serves as a consistent reminder of what to focus on to move you forward.

Have you ever created a vision board? Chances are you have done something similar, even if you didn't set out to make one on purpose. For example, have you ever done any of the following?:

- Hung family photos in a collection to remind you of who is important in your life
- Cut out pictures from magazines of clothes you wanted to wear (or be able to wear)
- Took photos of houses, boats, cars of other items that you wanted to have in the future
- Printed out information from websites of places you wanted to visit
- Taken photos with you to the hairstylist to show her what kind of haircut you wanted
- Written or cut out words or phrases you found motivating and wanted to remember
- Organized books on a shelf that you wanted to read in a place where you can see them
- Used Pinterest to collect photos or recipes of meals you wanted to make

I could go on and on! The point is, even if you don't feel you have created a vision board in the past, I am sure you have actually done something similar, and most likely you can relate to one of the above activities. The reason that you took this action is because you had a goal, however small in some cases, and you set about finding a visual way to remind yourself to accomplish it.

Let's apply this to your child. At the beginning of the chapter I asked you if any of the problems I listed resonated with you. If you said "yes" to even one, chances are your child could benefit from setting a goal that will give him a purpose. He will also benefit from creating a vision board to help him get focused on the goal and obtain it. What should that goal be? Well it depends on your child, and what you found out in Step 2 regarding his interests should really help you here.

Here are a few examples to get you started. In Step 2, your child expressed interest in (see words below in **bold**) and therefore his vision board would include (see examples from lists that follow):

- **Soccer** (insert any sport and adjust collection accordingly) - Perhaps he'd like to improve his game and therefore his vision board may include photos of famous soccer players, international team logos, ticket stubs to a soccer game, magazine cut-outs of soccer uniforms (or actual fabric of the team colors, or cut-out of an old uniform shirt) and the side of the box (where the name and image is) of the new cleats he just bought with his allowance.

- **Cook** – If your child loves to cook or bake, wants to make amazing meals or treats, and maybe even be a chef someday, then her vision board may include copies of choice recipes with photos of dishes she has made, pulled-out pages from recipe books and magazines, take-out menus from favorite restaurants, images from popular cooking magazines, photos of cakes she can't wait to attempt, details of cooking contests she wants to enter, or interviews of impressive chefs she admires.

- **Play guitar** (or other musical instrument) – If your child dreams of playing in a rock band or just loves to jam on a guitar, his vision board may include photos of famous guitar players, concert ticket stubs, used guitar strings, a guitar pick, sheet music of his favorite rock songs, images of guitars from magazines, and quotes from his favorite songs that are meaningful to him.

- **Draw** (or other creative activity) – If your child loves to draw and has goals of becoming an artist, her vision board may include some of her best smaller sketches, box top from the colored pencils she uses, ticket stubs from the local art museum, pamphlet or flyer from an art show featuring local artists' work, images of artists she admires, images of well-known paintings, quotes from notable artists or other meaningful and inspiring passages.

Let me state for the record again that parent modeling is going to go a long way here! Remember, what your child sees you do he will often imitate. If you have a respectful relationship with your child, he will respect what you value and spend time on. Therefore he will also come to value and potentially even spend time on the things that you do, just by modeling! So as your child creates a vision board for himself, why not create one of your own right alongside him? Alternatively, create your first one together that represents family goals and values, or an experience you'd like to have together, then let him create the next one for himself.

Caution: This gets addicting! Creator beware!

Materials needed (Available at Staples, Walmart, Office Depot and craft stores) :

(Choose 1) Poster board, cork board, foam board or binder with cardstock and plastic sheet covers

Stickers

Sticky substance – glue, glue stick, double sided tape, or thumb tacks for cork board

Art and craft supplies for decorating (optional but fun!) – markers, crayons, colored pencils, glitter, ribbon, beads, sequins, etc.

You collect:

Magazines, newspapers, pamphlets, flyers and other related materials you can cut up

Photos, images, pictures, other graphic designs

Ephemera – ticket stubs, programs, tags from clothing, leaflets, postcards, box tops, receipts, business cards, etc

You likely have:

Computer with printer - to print out photos, quotes, phrases, images, articles, etc.

Visit www.InnovativeReading.com for free resources!

Action steps - How to create a vision board

1. Begin by discussing the concept of a vision board with your child. You may plan to showcase the final product in his bedroom, or the reading nook you created in Step 3. Vision boards need to be kept in plain sight so that it reminds the owner of the vision created (the goals) every single day. If we hide it away, then it has no value.

2. Next, decide how you want to display the final product, what size you'd like it to be and what materials you'll use. For example, a cork board works great, and photos and images can be tacked up with thumb tacks and rearranged at any moment. For a more permanent product, consider poster board, or foam board and use tape or glue sticks to adhere the contents. (Many people even decoupage these for posterity!) I've also seen amazing vision boards made on 8x11 card stock pages, inserted into clear plastic sheet protectors and kept in a binder to be flipped through. While that is not completely out in the open, if the binder is easily accessible and you are short on wall space, this can work nicely as long as it's revisited often.

3. After you know the method for display and the size, start to collect resources with your child. At this stage in the collection process, there is no reason to be too picky. The goal is to have lots and lots of items to eventually choose from when it comes time to put the vision board together. Later on, your child can weed out what doesn't work. For now, gather any materials that seem to make sense. Sometimes the items that feel like a stretch work wonderfully when placed with other items to create a pleasing overall effect.

4. Look for images, photos, graphics, words, quotes and phrases that would work for this vision and ensure your child is heavily involved with you in this. Collect cut-outs from magazines, newspapers, pamphlets, flyers, stickers, ticket stubs, greeting cards, postcards, newsletters, box tops, and any kind of

ephemera that will help to stock the resource pile. This can take a while, from several days to a few weeks. No need to rush it; enjoy the process! Just don't forget to keep looking until you have quite a pile (consider the size of the board you want to fill.) You may want to find a cardboard box or plastic bin to keep it all in while you continue to search.

5. Once the pile is stocked with all kinds of options, that's when the real fun begins! At this point, you should have many more pieces than will fit on your board, so that your child can be choosy about what really goes into his vision for himself. After all, this vision will steer his focus and help him succeed in achieving an important goal. We want to be sure it's the best vision board it can be.

6. Let the magic begin! Your child should place the items and arrange, rearrange, and rearrange again until he has a pleasing display of words, phrases, quotes, images, photos and memorabilia on his vision board just the way he likes. At this point, he is ready to glue, tape or tack the pieces down to keep them there.

7. Want to get even more creative? Feel free to help your child add glitter, paint, marker, stickers, ribbons, fabric, felt, yarn, googly eyes, sequins or any other item to make it three dimensional, funky, and eye-catching.

8. Display in a prominent location. His bedroom wall is a great place so he sees it daily. Now step back and enjoy the masterpiece! Use this vision board to spark conversations about goals and life plans with your child. Revisit often.

Does this activity feel a little arts-and-craftsy? There is nothing wrong with that. In fact, it's a great project that shows you can have fun off-screens. Many children love the idea and process of creating vision boards. After all, it has to do with getting something that they want, and they get to create it. Don't approach this step with trepidation, or feel it needs to be perfect. Get excited, flex your imagination, and your child will be excited too.

Next steps, journaling:

So how did vision board creation go? If you thought it went smoothly, and your child was excited and can see the benefits, awesome! Kudos to you both for taking this on, and making something wonderful and inspiring for a long time to come. Additional vision boards can be produced for other goals and dreams; you don't need to stop at just one. Plus, she is ready to start journaling as the next step to imagining the life experiences she wants.

Why is this also important? When kids are creating vision boards and writing in their journals, they are not on screens. They are being creative with both words and images and accessing a part of their mind that screens never will.

If your child isn't that enthused, or is totally turned off by this activity, fear not! This may happen with some kids, especially those who steer away from crafts, or reading, or have a really hard time putting down the screens long enough to do anything else. I have you covered – be sure to check out the *Questions parents ask* section at the end of this chapter for what you can do next.

I am so excited you are now onto this part of Step 4! Quite honestly, journaling my goals has been the single most effective way I have stayed on track and accomplished my dreams by far! Let's get your child ready to write.

Here again it is important to model, so grab a journal of your own and write with your child for a few minutes daily if possible. Some families make this a practice just before breakfast, or bedtime, to ensure it gets done. Do what works for you.

Materials:

Journal with lines
Pen/pencil that feels good to write with
Optional (for decorating pages after writing): Stickers, crayons, colored pencils

How to start journaling:

- Allow your child to choose a notebook to function as a journal that she loves. It can be a simple spiral-bound notebook with lined pages or a marble composition notebook where the cover can be decorated. Or, spend a few more dollars and take a trip to the local bookstore to pick up a leather-bound or hardcover journal with a beautiful image or motivational words on the front. It really doesn't matter, as long as it inspires your child to write.

- Using your child's vision board for inspiration, have a conversation with her about putting those images into words. Continue the conversation about what goals your child has, why she has them and what steps she can take to get there. Keep the energy level up and be enthusiastic! This should not seem like work. Instead, writing down goals should be incredibly empowering. Help your child tap into that energy by feeling it yourself.

- State a few lines together out loud. Start by answering a few questions like, "What is my top interest right now? What do I want to do with that interest? How do I want to include it more in my life? How do I want to improve it and what steps can I take to get there? What have I already accomplished with this interest?" Let the pen start to capture some of the words in the answers – either in bullets, phrases or whole sentences.

- Journaling can be very free flowing, where the writer writes full paragraphs about her thoughts. Or it can be more scripted, especially for those who free-writing doesn't come to naturally. Determine which type of writing would suit your child.

- If the latter is your scenario, consider the *The 5 Minute Journal*, (see **Resources** section). In this guided notebook, the writer answers several questions on each page and doesn't have to work too hard to come up with what to say. Plus, the entire experience takes no more than 5 minutes a day but is still a very powerful practice.

- You can create your own "5 minute journal" for your child to follow by writing a few of these questions in her book and helping her answer them. Start by choosing just one or two and adding more (or make up your own together) as she gets more comfortable.

  ○ What are you grateful for today?

  ○ What big goal are you working on?

  ○ What interests do you want to pursue today?

  ○ What do you want to accomplish today?

  ○ What did you accomplish yesterday to move you towards your goal?

  ○ How did this make you feel?

  ○ Did you have any setbacks or frustrations?

  ○ What can you celebrate about yourself today/What are you proud of about yourself?

  ○ How can you help others today?

- Don't worry about how much your child is writing in her journal. Developing a journaling practice and stamina for writing takes time. For now, celebrate any writing and look to help her increase it slowly. Starting with conversations and reflecting on the vision board will help!

- Provide drawing utensils, stickers and other embellishments to add to the writing and let your child design the page as she gets inspiration to do so. Since I am not much of an artist, I love to add stickers to my writing. Embellishment is part of the fun!

Debbie and Arturo's Story - Montreal, Canada

Emma is our 10-year-old daughter. She was constantly watching YouTube and Netflix and was starting to get into social media in ways we didn't like. We were already worried and she was still so young. We couldn't even imagine how we were going to deal with this in high school. We decided not to wait to find out and get help sooner while it may be repairable. We reached out to Dr. Carroll and joined her program. We are SO thankful we did! Her advice really resonated with us and we implemented her ideas in a way that worked for our family, like she suggests. Emma's favorite part was when we got to the step with journaling and creating vision boards. It turns out, there's a reason she loves Instagram so much! She is highly visual and creative so making vision boards was a perfect outlet for her. Now she spends a lot more time collaging than on screens. This program helped make it happen. We never would have thought of this on our own!

Questions parents ask:
What if my child isn't interested in creating vision boards?

Although many children get excited about creating a vision board around something they love, some children are not all that interested, at least in the beginning. This is OK, and the following are a few ideas that may help. First, be sure you are modeling by making your own. You may ask your reluctant child to help you with yours instead of making his own first, or make a family one together (include your spouse and any other siblings) so everyone gets involved and it's meaningful to all. Hang this in a prominent location and refer to it often. This may be enough to inspire your child. Continue to collect the materials anyway for your child's vision board and suggest he do the same. Children often love this step. When you have plenty of materials, making a vision board is the next obvious action. Even if you just get to handling the materials and discussing what they represent, you are doing great! (If creating the board is too much, you can even keep them in a shoe box for him to look at on occasion.) Suggest you make a vision board together as a rainy or cold day activity, when it feels like there is nothing else better to do (and gaming is not the other option – see last chapter on setting boundaries).

I am still not sure what to collect for vision board creation. It seems overwhelming. Any suggestions?

The first time you create a vision board it may feel overwhelming. However, the trick is to start where you are and just get going! Do you have a pile of magazines or newspapers laying around? Just start cutting them up. Use whatever materials you have and do not try to be perfect. No one else is going to see the final product and its sole purpose is to inspire your child to pursue his dreams off screens. Follow the guidelines as I have explained them above and you will see it's rather easy and lots of fun.

What if my child doesn't want to journal?

Many children say they hate to write. Interestingly, journaling is often the practice that helps them change this sentiment. It's worth making an effort to get your child there. Here again, parent modeling is key. Let your child see you enjoying your own journal at least a few times a week. Try to entice her to write just a little by using one of the prompts I provided earlier, or go with *The 5 Minute Journal* that does most of the work for you. Encourage your child to draw more than write, and use stickers, paint, colored pencils or pens, glue and any other medium that makes it more fun. If the idea of a bound journal is too much, use a different sheet of brightly colored paper instead to write and draw on and eventually they can be tied or stapled together.

What if my child wants to write and draw about other topics in the journal besides goals and interests?

By all means, let her. If she is writing and inventing and not asking for a screen, that is a huge celebratory moment! Let her creative juices flow. You can always consider separate journals down the road if she'd like one solely for art or stories rather than the more standard journal entry. For now, go with it! She is writing, dreaming and using her imagination.

Joe and Jackie's Story – Carlsbad, CA

By age 11, Martin wanted to be on screens all day. We didn't ever see screens as a problem, until they were. And then they really were. Martin became bored by anything and everything else unless he was playing a video game. Family time? No interest. School? Boring. Friends? Stopped seeing them. Church group? Don't care! Reading?

Never! The only thing he ever seemed to have any interest in once in a while was an electric guitar we got him for his 11th birthday. Still, most days that just sat in the corner. Needless to say, as his parents, we were now very concerned.

We saw Dr. Carroll speaking at an event and thought perhaps she had some ideas we could use with Martin. We weren't sure how he'd take to some of the ideas she suggested, however, because Martin wasn't open to anything. But we decided to give it a shot, as we had nothing to lose except to let our son slide further down the slope into screen addiction – something we weren't willing to do without a fight.

As parents, we got on the same team, which we found was critical, as we implemented Dr. Carroll's steps. It was a slow and steady process but after several weeks things began to improve. At one point we had considered some extreme measures, such as switching him to a screen-free school environment, or maybe sending him to a summer camp detox program but we now feel less drastic steps are necessary if we keep implementing this system. What a relief to feel like we are getting our son back.

FREE BONUS QUIZ!

Is Your Child

Hooked on Screens?

http://bit.ly/screentimequiz

Chapter 5

Step 5 - Design Life Experiences Through Adventures

Once you learn to read you will be forever free.

Frederick Douglas

Bryan always seemed bored unless he was on a screen. To be honest, although my wife and I drove him around to lots of activities, we never really made family time a priority. Since we believed Bryan needed help to put down the screens, we signed up for Dr. Carroll's program and we learned that we, as parents, needed a lot of help too. In Step 5 we learned the importance of planning fun adventures and once we started to do this, we can't believe we waited so long. Now we take screen-free day trips AND read about them in advance. Not only does Bryan enjoy the trips as well as the reading part, but so does our younger son, Reggie. My wife and I do as well. It's amazing that one piece of advice has completely transformed our family dynamic.
Marc Z. Upper Saddle River, NJ

Problem:

Your child has no enthusiasm for reading and doesn't feel it's relevant to her life. She sees no reason to read and therefore says she's not interested no matter what book you try to offer her. Any which way you slice it, Instagram wins.

OR

You may take family trips and plan fun events but it's a hit or miss that the kids even care when you get there. How can you increase their excitement over real life experiences and make them at least as interesting as the screens they won't stop staring at?

What this step is about:

Use your child's interests and goals to determine what he wants to know more about. Entice him to read about it, and then share the experience. Read about the adventure first, then go create the family experiences that your child will remember for a lifetime. They don't have to be expensive, overly time-consuming or include far-away travel. They do need to be real, authentic time together that your child finds interesting.

Benefits:

Too often today screens replace actual life experiences. Children turn to social media and video games for the excitement they offer, even though it's virtual. This form of entertainment provides instant gratification in a world where parents are often too busy to make good old-fashioned fun with their kids a priority. Parents who provide tangible experiences that are interesting to their children report that their kids are less fascinated by screens, read more, play more, communicate better and enjoy family time.

In addition, children who have real-life opportunities do better in school, are more verbally expressive, are stronger readers and writers, are well-rounded, are better able to understand their world and communicate well with others. Wow!

Plus (and it's a BIG plus!) when kids get excited about something, they are more likely to be open to reading about it. Eventually they may even ask to read about it, because they want to learn more and get ready for the opportunity ahead.

How to do it:

Who doesn't love a day trip to the zoo, the ballpark, a hike in the woods or the ice skating rink? What about a space museum, an aquarium, a high school musical, or a Civil War reenactment? (See the **Resources** section for dozens of more ideas for fun and free or low-cost activities.) While these excursions are enjoyable as standalone experiences, what makes them even more interesting once you get there is knowing some facts, statistics, or other pertinent information before you arrive.

For example, it's SO much better to go to the zoo and visit the monkey house after you have read up on some facts about different types of monkeys and their interesting behavior. (For starters you can actually identify the varied species instead of just gawking!) It's way better to go see a play or musical if you understand the storyline in advance, know the words to a few of the songs and even a couple of fun facts about the theater if it's historical. And Civil War reenactments can be fascinating if you go armed with knowledge about what the soldiers wore during that time period, what the weapons were like and how rough the weather conditions were during the important battles. Has your family ever been to one of these events or places and frankly were a little *b-o-r-e-d?* I bet it's because you didn't know much about it to begin with.

I have proven this to myself over and over again in life and continue to find it's true. Recently, for example, my husband and I went to see the Broadway musical, Hamilton. I didn't know any details of the story, but I went and had a lovely time. The costumes were incredible, the dancing and songs were amazing, but I found myself wishing I knew more about that time in history so the words to the songs made more sense. I could remember a little about what I learned in high school but that was a long time ago!

I loved the play so much that it inspired me to research the time period in American history and read as much as I could about the musical, the era, and Lin Manuel Miranda, the playwright. I was hooked! I found the information so interesting that I just had to go back and see the musical again through the lens of all this new knowledge I had!

Several months later I had the opportunity to see it a second time and I was totally amazed at how much better I understood what I was experiencing. Nuances in the words stood out to me, the lyrics were so much funnier now that I caught the hidden jokes, puns and contrasts that I totally missed the first time. I even learned a few pieces of trivia about the Richard Rodgers Theatre on Broadway that increased my appreciation for the venue. The experience was waaaaay better since I spent some time learning about the play and its historical context. It convinced me even more about the importance of Step 5.

Has this ever happened to you? My guess is you can remember a time when you appreciated an experience so much more than you would have otherwise because you were armed with knowledge. Can you think of a time this has happened for your child as well? If not, I highly suggest you do a little experiment and try it out! You will be completely sold on reading up before a family adventure when you see the difference it makes in the enjoyment level. And remember the big plus here, it gets your child reading books and off screens.

The challenges with adventures

We are all pulled in so many directions today, that we often fail to make time for fun events that allow us to spend an afternoon with family and connect to the world around us, other people, and new places.

Weekdays are packed with work and school, after school events and activities, doctor appointments, music lessons, religious studies, and endless hours of homework. Dinner needs to be cooked and eaten, lunches packed and clothes readied for the next day, and now I want you to model reading every night (Remember Step 1)! There is just no time for anything else.

So, what do your weekends look like? Have you overscheduled those too, finding no time for high-quality family outings because everyone is running in a million, low-quality directions? Maybe some weekends need to be like that, but do all weekends?

Consider what you might actually say "no" to. Then do it to free yourselves and replace low-quality activity with high-quality family time. Does any of this sound familiar to you?

- You accept invitations to birthdays, showers, weddings, fund-raisers and other events that you really don't want to attend

- You volunteer for the bake sale, car wash, PTA or charity event even when you are already short on time and your heart is not really in it

- You run errands all weekend – dry cleaning, walking the dog, veterinary appointments, haircuts, trips to the post office, clothes shopping, buying presents, filling prescriptions, getting the oil changed or going to the bank, even though there are apps or other people who can take care of most of them for you (It really is true, you just need to set it up!)

- You accept dinner invitations from couples you would rather not hang out with (Really, break up with them already!)

- You run your children around to activities that they or you are not very enthusiastic about (Another rainy day at Chucky Cheese? Ugh!)

- You spend your weekend cleaning the house, mowing the lawn, paying the bills, doing loads of laundry and other mundane tasks and might be able to skip it, automate it, cut it back, reschedule it, or outsource it instead

  You make several trips to the grocery store each week, and wait on line to check out (Try a delivery or meal shipping service already! Many have free or inexpensive delivery costs. See **Resources** section for examples)

- You find yourself watching TV, Facebook, or YouTube videos to zone out and can lose track of this time pretty easily

When parents work with me we look at their schedules and all the events that happen in a family's week. Most people will tell me they have zero ability to cut anything out, yet when we go through the activities together one at a time, we *always* find two, three or more that can either be cut back substantially, delegated to someone else easily or just taken right off the to-do list. Parents are shocked and thrilled at this discovery, and it sometimes takes a fresh pair of eyes to see it. We usually find several hours of hidden time a week that can be better spent with family. Be tough with yourself, unapologetic, and edit ruthlessly. The only time we have is now. Time with your family is worth it and cannot be retrieved once it's spent on sub-standard activities.

Let's recoup some of that time and spend it on a planned adventure.

Adventures come in all shapes and sizes. For our purposes here, I am going to be talking about weekend-types of adventures that need a little more time, just to prove a point. Be open-minded in your own planning! You may not have weekends off, or have some other reason to schedule your adventure on a weekday or evening so go ahead and do it! What matters most is that you DO IT.

The experience you design can be far away, and those are awesome! However, life is usually too busy to do that often and so if we stick to options closer to home, we can get many more adventures in. (Yippee!) Additionally, if we keep the time commitment and expenses down, then planning these excursions won't seem like much of a big deal and can be freely enjoyed due to less stress.

The most important thing is that whatever you decide to do, the adventurers (that's you and your kids!) are excited about it and read up on it first. Deal?

Action steps:

1.　Choose an adventure that will interest your child. It may be helpful if it correlates to something on the vision board (but that's not imperative). For example, if your child has photos of baseball players on his vision board because he wants to get better at his swing and make the JV team at school, then an adventure to a batting cage, or ballpark to watch a pro game is perfect! Whatever you choose, be sure it ties into an interest your child has expressed (see Step 2).

2. Choose the date this adventure will take place and commit. Clear the calendar for that date, and let everyone know this is happening.

3. Decide with your child what else you both want to know about this topic before you go. If you will be visiting a pro game, for example, does he want to learn more about the team you are going to see? If so, read up on the players, their stats and the line-up. What about the actual ball park? Is it new? Historical? How many seats does it have? When was it built? What other fascinating facts about it can you find? How about baseball in general? It's the good ole, all-American pastime so you can bet there will be loads of books written about it. Ask a librarian to pull several for you to pick up on your way home. I always suggest including at least one illustrated book, even for older kids. In the baseball example, be sure to include the illustrated book, *Baseball Saved Us* by Ken Mochizuki for an eye-opening look at how baseball played a role in the life of a Japanese-American child in a Japanese internment camp in the 1940s. (Bonus for this type of read aloud - You'll not only make a literacy connection to baseball but learn about history as well.)

Helpful hint: Remember that any reading is good reading for this purpose, so long as it's age-appropriate and on-topic. Try to find a variety of resources, such as picture books and chapter books, along with articles, flyers, pamphlets, guidebooks, customer reviews and anything that is written. Authentic reading is the best kind and will help your child learn how to conduct real-world research for his future trips as he grows up.

4. Talk about what you learned and what you want to be sure you experience on your adventure. You can even add to your vision boards if you feel moved to do so.

5. Go do it!

Lorna's Story – Reno, NV

I didn't think I could get my two kids interested in anything physical. They were so absorbed by screens at the ages of 10 and 12 that I was beginning to lose hope. It was evident that video games and social media were the easy way out for their personal entertainment. Exercise of any kind seemed like a lost cause! However, I decided to band together with another mom and implement Step 5. We took the kids on a day hike but first we read about the animals and tracks we might encounter on the trail. The fact that animals were involved got my kids interested, and they agreed to do some research of their own both on and off the computer. The day of the hike they enjoyed looking for (and actually spotted!) some of the wildlife they had read about. We were thrilled and all had a wonderful day. I will definitely plan more of these "adventures"!

Questions parents ask:
Can't we read online about our event? It's so much faster to Google everything and read that way!

My answer is yes, and no. Of course, you can Google anything and get all the information you'll ever need. And yes, reading websites is still reading. In addition, it may be a challenge to find non-website type material on your topic. So, if that is true for you, my recommendation is to print some of the information off the computer and read it on paper (try the printer-friendly version, many websites have that option). Once it is on paper, you can write on it, highlight it, underline words or ideas of interest, staple several sheets together to create a "guidebook" and have it to take with you on your trip.

The idea is to minimize screen time. So if you can find real books, paper pamphlets, newspaper articles or other non-screen reading, that is the best way to go. The key is to be always on the lookout and start a collection of fun information that may lead to upcoming trips of interest for your family.

In addition, if the research must be done on a screen, have that count towards daily screen time. At least it is better for the brain than video games! You can find more on my recommendations for that in chapter 6.

I feel overwhelmed by how to collect reading materials. I don't have the time or the resources to find what to read about. What should I do?

You don't need a ton of reading materials for each adventure. To keep it simple while still accomplishing the goal, limit it to one book, one article (that you Googled online and printed out) and maybe a pamphlet or flyer for each trip. Once you feel this is doable, you can later expand your resources for each additional adventure. Don't let your intimidation of collecting resources be the reason you don't accomplish this step. Keep it simple! Three helpful hints on this are:

1. Keep an eye out for related articles as you do your own reading. You'd be surprised at what you come across in magazines and newspapers that are relevant once you pay attention.

2. Reuse resources. Did you find a book or article on the best day hikes in your area? That's a keeper! You might use it over and over again for many adventures you plan if your family decides that hiking, trail walking, snowshoeing, cross country skiing, rock collecting, bird watching, stream fishing, or animal, scat and track identification are on your to-do list!

3. I don't want to sound like a broken record but… Find a helpful librarian and utilize her. This is exactly what she does!

FREE BONUS QUIZ!

Is Your Child

Hooked on Screens?

http://bit.ly/screentimequiz

Chapter 6

Monitoring and Setting Boundaries

When people declared, "Your kids must love the iPad!"
Steve Jobs answered, "Actually we don't allow the iPad in our
home. We think it's too dangerous for them."

We bought our daughter a cell phone in elementary school because we thought it would keep her safe. Little did we know all the problems it would soon cause the whole family. We heard Dr. Carroll speak at a school function and just knew we needed to follow her advice if we wanted to help Casey and stop the constant arguing. We are so thankful she shared her 5 steps with us. Our family is making great progress away from screen addiction and we look forward to spending time with each other again. Dawn and Mike R. Lansing, MI.

Wow! I am impressed! You have read this far and you are still going. That's great! Both your children and your household will be so much better and healthier if you implement the strategies we have discussed. I know it hasn't been easy either. There was a lot to learn, a lot to do, and all of it requires a commitment to consistency. Don't worry about being perfect. It's not about that. It's about taking small, effective steps and making an effort each day.

Two critical elements to managing the technology in your home are how to monitor and set boundaries around screen-time. Although these practices should be happening while you are working on the 5 steps, they deserve their own chapter because of the importance to not only your child's health as it pertains to screens, but also his safety in general. While I could write an entire book on this topic, I will explain with enough depth here to give you a solid start on what to do in your home right now to both protect your family and give my 5 step system a turbo boost in effectiveness.

Problem: The world wide web is just that, worldly and very wide. Way more so than we'd like our youth to take in. How can parents allow kids appropriate screen experiences while ensuring their safety and preserving their innocence?

You need the strategies and tools to help keep you informed of what your child is doing online. You also need to lay down guidelines that will ensure your child knows there are rules for screen use in your family and for good reason!

Benefits:

By implementing these strategies your stress will decrease and your confidence will increase as a parent in the digital age. Plus, your children will be safer and happier. (They may not agree with the happy part in the beginning!)

Keep your kids healthy and safe. Protect their minds and ensure they spend time on other, healthier pursuits.

How to do it:
Monitoring screens

My kids accuse my wife and me of being fascists and overly concerned about tech, and they say that none of their friends have the same rules. That's because we have seen the dangers of technology firsthand. I've seen it in myself, I don't want to see that happen to my kids.

Chris Anderson, CEO 3D Robotics

The simple definition of monitoring your child's screens means to watch what your child is doing while she is on the device, and also check up on what your child has been doing in their accounts (like social media) after they are off the screen. Depending on the age of the child this can be challenging, and you may be met with varying degrees of resistance. Therefore, it's important that you talk to your child about why you are monitoring his screen use. Let's take it step by step.

Why should you monitor your child's screen use?

This one is a no-brainer but I'm going to say it anyway. The internet is like the wild, wild west. Anything and everything goes. There is violence, foul language, hate, intolerance, bigotry, lurking child molesters and lots of pornography, all quite easily accessible (even by accident) for those who are not careful about monitoring. As a parent, you want to keep your child safe and you also want to filter what he sees. Children grow up soon enough. Let's protect them while they are still young. In addition, if they know you are monitoring their use, they'll feel safer and are more likely to be careful themselves and tell you if something negative does slip through.

Ways you can monitor your child's screen use

For younger children through the 'tween years, screens should be used in the main rooms of the home only. That means screens in bedrooms, basement playrooms and loft hideaways are not advised. Parents need to be around in order to easily see and hear what children are watching and doing online and in games. Many parents will approve only certain apps, websites, software programs and videos for children to watch and interact with, and ensure periodically that they are the only ones downloaded on the device their child uses. Savvy parents also check the history of the screen's use in order to tell what children have actually been on and to ensure that any parental monitoring software that may be installed is actually doing its job properly. Passwords can be set so that the parent must sign the child on and off the device. These steps help safeguard your younger child while using screens and gives you more of the control, where it belongs.

As children get into their teen years it can be really hard to keep them in front of you on screens. They'll have homework they need to do on a computer and will need a quiet place they can concentrate. It's likely they'll want more liberal access to social media sites and games. This is when parental monitoring software becomes critical. Many parents are surprised at what their kids get into online when left unattended. Don't think your child won't venture off and be curious about what's out there. She will. Internet trolls and evil people work hard to lure kids in unsuspectingly to hate sites, porn sites, sites that glorify depression, cutting and eating disorders, and get young people addicted to video games. It's better to have your child mad at you over tightly monitored screens than some of the terrible alternatives.

While those may be extreme examples, other more benign but still unhealthy options exist in even greater numbers. Teens routinely engage in unkind social media threads with friends or acquaintances from school. This quickly turns into bullying and ostracizing peers, especially since it's much easier to hide behind a screen and say mean words than it is in person. Kids don't always understand the hurt they can cause by what they write. Endless hours are spent by school administrators in every middle and high school in America attempting to resolve online conflicts, repair broken friendships, and mitigate the damage teens do to each others' reputations - usually with little success.

Many kids feel depressed when viewing various photos of "perfect" looks, lives or families on Instagram, Facebook and Snapchat. These sites push unrealistic images of life, bodies, relationships and material objects that lead to personal comparisons of kids to their peers while playing on their emotions. Unchecked social media use by 'tweens and teens has led to more bullying, social isolation, depression, sexting and even suicide than the world has previously known. There are countless reasons why it's imperative to closely monitor your child's screens for as long as you can.

There are many different types of parent monitoring software programs out there and they run the gamut in what they can do for you. The basic controls cover content (to filter the bad stuff from the internet), and many allow you to set time limits on usage. You can get software that monitors social media activity, lets you know when your child has attempted to access a blocked website or app, and some even allow you to remotely manage the security so you can tweak as needed, even if you are not home. With all of these options, it may take a little research, but finding the right solution will be a gift once you own and install it.

Social media trackers can be especially helpful to parents of 'tweens and teens, however they require that your child share the passwords with you. This may feel like an invasion of privacy to some kids, so it is very important you not only explain what you are doing to keep them safe but why you are doing it. There are an untold number of horror stories of child abduction and molestation that have happened with help from the internet. You can find them with a quick Google search if you need proof that the world isn't always the pretty place that Instagram would have you believe.

You can monitor each device separately, or purchase one system for the home that monitors them all. My research shows that a home network device is a simple solution, however it won't be as robust as individual device controls. Also take note, kids today are way more tech-smart than most parents. (Sorry, but you know it's true.) Be aware that many kids may make efforts to get around these parental controls and with enough talent and persistence, will be successful. This is another reason why having frank conversations with your child early and often is critical. You want them to buy-in to their safety, not work around you.

Talk to your child

If you start to monitor screen use without a family discussion, chances are the kids are going to stage a mini-rebellion. That's because they need to feel included in the new rules, and have a say in them. Kids need to feel safe, but they also need to have a voice. It will benefit the whole process if you sit the family down (maybe during a device-free dinner) and think through together what appropriate screen monitoring will look like for everyone. Then, be sure to write down what you agreed upon and hang it in a conspicuous spot. You'll want a constant reminder so that no one forgets the importance of screen safety and how the family is ensuring it for all members.

For information on parental control software products, check the *Resources* section.

Questions parents ask:
What screens should I allow in the home?

This is a personal question and every family will answer it differently. While I do have strict recommendations around where the screens should be used and for how long, it's hard to tell parents which screens they should or should not own. However, in general, I don't advocate buying elementary-aged children any device of their own. I recommend family-use tablets and laptops until at least middle school, and then extra close monitoring of all devices once children have a device of their own. What apps kids are on, what games they are playing and what videos they are watching is a far more important question. If waiting until middle school or beyond to purchase devices for kids doesn't work for your family, then stick to close monitoring and strong vetting of content no matter who owns the device. In addition, see my guidelines on how to keep a Reader-Friendly Home™ in Step 3.

At what age should my child own a cell phone?

This is a tricky question for sure! It's hard to give the perfect age. No one can argue the security a cell phone gives you as a parent, being able to call your child to know where she is, or have him call you in case of any emergency. The convenience factor alone often seems worth giving them a phone rather young. After all, we know kids can figure out how to use them!

Note, however, that Silicon Valley executives, Steve Jobs and Bill Gates didn't advocate giving their children cell phones (or tablets) until well into their teens. (In fact many go so far as to send their children for tech-free private education such as to Waldorf Schools.) They had strong reasons, and they are the gurus in this field. They want to protect their kids from the dangers of technology and so do you.

Smartphones are incredibly hard to monitor when they are as small as an index card. Once you put a smartphone in a child's possession, parents say it is nearly impossible for the child to put it down. Therefore, the longer you wait to give your child a personal smartphone the better. Though they are not nearly as cool, old school flip phones and the Gizmo Pal do work for making phone calls if that is what you really want your child to be able to do.

My child gets angry/annoyed/argumentative about me monitoring his screens. What can I do?

Monitoring screens without conversations with your child may lead to their rebelling, especially if this practice is new in the home. This is why getting your child on-board with it first is critical. Be sure to have discussions early and often about why you are monitoring, what you are monitoring for, and the real-world consequences if you didn't monitor. Discuss your family values and let your child contribute to the conversation. Come up with a plan together for the monitoring and you might even allow him to be involved in choosing the software program you use. Be sure to model good behaviors as well. Your child will probably figure out if you are making bad choices online while telling him to do the opposite.

Setting Boundaries Around Screen Time

"We limit how much technology our kids use at home."

Steve Jobs

Problem: Step into the era of screens without setting limits around them in your home and suddenly everyone in the family is walking around the house, staying up way too late, and practically showering with their cell phones! While you know screens are the way of the world and don't want you or your kids to live without them, you think, "Come on already, can't we even have a decent conversation at dinnertime? And why are we texting each other when we're only three feet apart?!"

While monitoring screen time is more about safety, setting boundaries for screen use ensures children have time for other healthy activities. Boundaries set kids up for success because they clearly know what is allowed and what is not allowed in terms of time and place. Here as well, you want to be sure you include your child in the planning and discussion of the boundaries you set. It's critical it works for your family, and that you can be consistent about implementing them. Inconsistent application and unrealistic expectations of boundaries will be the reasons they fail. Be consistent and keep it real and you will succeed.

The first thing you need to decide is how much time a day is appropriate for each child. This will differ depending on how old your children are. The American Academy of Pediatrics recommends (at the time of this printing) no more than one hour a day of screens for children ages 2-5. For children over the age of 6, they recommend parents use their best judgement and limit their use to ensure other healthy and productive activities are taking place. By the way, they recommend absolutely no screens for children 18 months and younger.

When considering how much time is enough for each child, I have a few other recommendations. Children are getting a lot of screen time in most schools these days. While you can argue that this time is used for educational purposes and kids are learning during that time, they are still on a screen and - particularly if they are playing any kind of game (educational included) - it is effecting their brain. Children are still being artificially stimulated, as well as exposed to blue light (which is disruptive to sleep even when absorbed in the afternoon) and radiation. While the jury is still out on just how harmful the radiation may be, no doubt it's best to keep it to a minimum.

In addition, screen use begets more desire for same. So when trying to decide how much online time is appropriate at home, I suggest parents find out how much screen time is happening at school in each grade level, and learn what classrooms are using it for. If you disagree with the amount of time spent on screens or the reason they are on the devices, have a conversation with your child's teacher or school administrator.

The second consideration is how your child acts directly after each screen use, and after cumulative use – say over a week's time. Is your child over-stimulated, angry, acting depressed or aggressive after a short period of time on screens? If so, more time will not help these behaviors and can make them worse.

If, however, screen use doesn't seem to have an impact on your child's personality or behavior, she might be able to handle more time, especially if used productively, for example, to create a piece of music, collect photos to print for a vision board, or write in an online journal. Many children have a much better temperament after using screens to create something – like graphic art or writing, than they do after they play video games or watch an aggressive movie.

After you decide on time, another consideration is when in the day it is appropriate to use that time. For example, during the week, do you want your child to get homework finished and set the dinner table before any recreational screen use? Are you concerned that screens will keep your child from a sound sleep and therefore want them shut down an hour before bedtime? (That's a great opportunity to promote reading instead!)

On weekends, would you rather your child be outdoors during daylight hours getting sunshine and exercise? Perhaps limit screen use to a few evening hours, say, before the family gathers to watch a movie together. If there are chores to be done, should they get done first before screens are allowed? These are all questions to consider as you discuss with your spouse and children what responsible screen use in your house should look like.

Once you have thought through the above considerations, feel free to chat with other parents about what they are doing at home and what seems to work for them. You may find that many parents are quite thoughtful about screen time and have established boundaries that are working very well. You don't have to re-invent the wheel. Just ask questions and try out a few ideas. You will eventually find boundaries that work for the family and allow your children to spend time on healthy activities.

Once you have your boundaries set, create a family contract that outlines them clearly and that everyone signs. Hang it in a location where everyone can see it easily and refer to it often. Hold each other accountable! You might even consider repercussions that apply to anyone who slips (that includes you, mom and dad). For example, was someone gaming before chores? He gets an extra chore that day. How about texting at dinner? Maybe she loses her phone for the rest of the evening. You decide what works in your house and if everyone keeps a sense of humor while understanding the importance of sticking to the rules, then the accountability part can be fun.

Other boundaries to consider:

Length of use is important, but so is location. This, of course, is going to vary from family to family and again I stress you need to do what works for you in order to ensure consistency. I have made some strong recommendations to help you not let screens take over the house. Make changes as necessary but don't give in too easily either. Stand your ground, be the parent, and follow through with your decision. In addition, don't forget modeling! If you say no screens allowed at the dinner table, then please do not take out your cell phone for "just one important email". Your kids will call you out on it and you'll have lost credibility.

Questions parents ask:
Where should screens be allowed at home?

For younger children through grade school, they should only be allowed in common areas in the home. Living room, family room, dining room (during non-meal times) or kitchen. Remember you want to be able to see and hear what your child is doing at all times with just a quick glance or check-in. If he is in his bedroom or the basement gameroom, you can't do that unless you decide to hang out with him there. My guess is you don't have time for that!

For older kids in middle and high school, this gets trickier. If your child has his own cell phone, it's not practical to tell him he can never take it to his bedroom. After all, the device was made small for the exact reason that it's supposed to be carried around. Kids really take that seriously! In addition, homework often gets done on computers, Chromebooks and even tablets in bedrooms so that they can be in a quiet place to study. My suggestion is to take advantage of the monitoring software I mention in the **Resources** section so you can control the usage no matter where your child is in the home. You can program the software so that he can't actually use the computer or phone for anything but studying until the time is appropriate.

Pass the cell phone basket:

Meal time should be family time whenever possible. Even if every family member can't be present for dinner, those that can eat together should also talk together. Therefore, set up a cell phone basket that everyone contributes their device to at meal time. Put it in another room and make sure the ringers are off! Commit to eating at least a few meals together as a family each week and talk to each other about what is going on in your lives, what you are looking forward to (adventures!) and what you think you want to pursue (vision board!). When the meal is over, it's up to you if everyone can have their phone back right away, but at least keep meal-time phone free.

The best advice to help ensure kids get a good night sleep is to collect all cell phones before bedtime. Most kids, if they can get away with it, would spend hours each night playing Minecraft, scrolling through social media feeds or texting friends who are also still awake at all hours. If your child has a cell phone in her room at night, there is a good chance this is happening whether you know it or not. After all, you're exhausted and probably sleeping soundly! Many parents have told me they have found their child up at 2 am, hiding a cell phone or iPad under the blanket while texting away or staring zombie-eyed at a gaming screen.

Kids need sleep. They need it even more during the teen years. When kids are on screens for even just a little while at night, the blue light suppresses melatonin production, disrupting their ability to get a good night's sleep. Cognitive stimulation is another issue. The brain is unable to wind down when on a device because it's being wound up! When this happens night after night, there is a real adverse effect on the child's health and the ability to succeed in school is impaired.

Lack of sleep also alters mood and behaviors. In addition, cell phones make all sorts of noises. Unless it's put in airplane mode or shut down completely, it's inevitable that some app is going to ring, beep, flash, ping or vibrate which will disrupt sleep. (I know this from too many of my own sleepless nights until I learned how to control it.) If the phone is off or in airplane mode, then it might as well be out of the room. Round up all phones (and tablets) at night and keep them in a parent's closet.

Devices in the car:

Many families that I work with have established a car reading basket. It stays in the car and is meant to keep kids occupied on shorter trips, or for the first hour or more of a longer car trip. It often includes a new book, favorite magazines, and appropriate car games that are not screen-based, such as Mad-Libs. I like the practice, especially for grade school children, that screens are not allowed for short trips, or the first hour at least of longer trips. If they need to be occupied they must pull from the basket, or play a game like I-Spy. Once the hour is up, they may go to a screen for the designated time that they would usually get at home (so no more than an hour for ages 2-5 and whatever you designated for older than that) unless they are watching a family-friendly movie. After the movie or the time is up, they go back to the basket for another hour and the process repeats itself.

This may work too for older kids or you may need to adjust. You might try an audio book that everyone can get into for kids in the older elementary grades and up. A mix of screen and off-screen time is highly recommended for all kids on longer car trips!

Devices at restaurants, or other public places:

There was a time before screens when prepared parents took their children out to dinner, or church, or other place where quieter behavior was preferred and brought along favorite toys, books, puzzles, crayons and crafts. I can remember my older sister with her three children (who are 25, 22 and 19 right now) always schlepping a bag of portable activities to keep her children occupied. Some people used to think that was too much effort and wondered why she did it, but everyone admired how "well-behaved" her kids were when they were out. All three kids went on to graduate either salutatorian or valedictorian of high school, got into highly competitive colleges on scholarships and are avid readers even still.

Is there a correlation between the bag of books she hefted all over back then and the success of all three children? We'll never know. But I will say, it didn't hurt! I tell this story to illustrate that yes, an iPad is lighter and easier to carry to keep your child occupied than a whole bag of games. But it isn't the only option on the go. The bottom line is this. If you use a cell phone or tablet at the restaurant to occupy your child so you can have a peaceful dinner, I totally get it. Just be sure to count that towards the day's total screen time hours. However, consider what one mom said to me, "We go out to dinner as a treat to enjoy each other's company so if we spend the time on screens, we might as well save the money and stay home!" I like her style.

What is your personal opinion on how long my child should be on screens each day?

I agree with the AAP on screens for children ages 2-5 in that no more than an hour a day is appropriate. Personally, I'd like to see children in that age group have days where they are not on a screen at all, and some days where they are on for no more than 30 minutes. If children age 5 and under are insisting to be on a screen, I'd love to see you working to stimulate them in other healthier ways such as getting outside for a ballgame, reading, cooking together or experiencing nature. Their young brains are very malleable and they can be highly affected by screen use.

Depending on your child and the use at school, I would argue that 1-2 hours a day for elementary school children and no more than 2 hours a day for older children (through teen years) of recreational screen time is plenty. The hard part is once a teen gets a cell phone, screen use becomes "constantly intermittent". They may be on and off it several times in 10 minutes, so it's hard to add up that time (know anyone else like that?). Here again it's important to engage your child in non-screen activities to ensure they do something else long enough to not be checking the cell phone every 5 minutes. Finally, if you notice that screens negatively impact your child's mood or behavior and you are staying within the guidelines above, you may want to work towards even less time, or break the time up throughout the day. Your child will need your help to navigate this and it won't be easy. However, his mental health may depend on it.

What if my child won't give up the cell phone during dinner, or overnight, no matter what I say?

It is imperative to have discussions with your children about why you are setting these rules, and include them in the rule-making. Parents need to model the same behaviors they expect from children and put the 5 steps of my system into place to engage your child in other productive activities as often as possible. If you find you have done all of this consistently and your child is still seriously resistant to putting down the electronic devices long enough to engage in other healthy activities, I strongly urge you to seek additional help through one of the resources I provide in this book (see **Resources** section), or an outside counselor who understands screen addiction.

Note: You could try to take the cell phone away for a length of time and that can work temporarily. But living in a world without cell phones is not realistic today and your relationship with your child may suffer. It is better to get outside counseling to help you understand the root of the problem, and help your child develop a healthy relationship with devices that he'll need for future success.

Chapter 7

Parent Interviews - Moms Talk About Challenges and Making it Work

If it's any consolation to being a parent in the screen-age, you are certainly not alone! Just about every parent is dealing with similar challenges around managing screens with their children and helping them navigate the world where digital devices threaten to take over all other interests and activities.

Meet three moms that are just like you with children who love their screens. Here we chat about what they are struggling with as a parent of digital natives, their fears and concerns, and about trying some of the steps in my book. Each of them value reading and want their screen-loving children to read books.

Parent Interview 1: Nancy D. - East Greenwich, RI

Colleen: I am so pleased that I have Nancy with me here today. Nancy is a mom of two: a teen and a 'tween! She is also Area Coordinator for BOKS in Rhode Island which stands for Build Our Kids' Success. It's an initiative of the Reebok Foundation, and is a free physical activity program that gets children moving, activating their brains for learning. I like the sound of that! Nancy, tell us where you are from and about your children.

Nancy: I live in East Greenwich, Rhode Island. My husband and I have a 14-year-old daughter and a 10-year-old son.

Colleen: Let's talk first about screens and their usage at home. Do your children use screens? If so, what screens do they use, and what does that look like in your home?

Nancy: My daughter is a freshman in high school. She had been using a Chromebook for middle school, and she has an iPhone that I handed down to her. My son, who is in 5th grade, does not have a phone yet. He has a Kindle, which he uses for games. And I have to say, my husband and I have been late to the party regarding cell phones and games. I think our daughter was one of the last kids of her peer group to get a phone.

We felt it was time for her to get a phone in middle school when it was helpful to us that she have one. When we needed to be able to reach her, for example, and get her a message about pick-up after cross country practice or another after school activity. We didn't want her to get a phone when it was really all about texting, and Instagram, the social piece of it, because that's a murky area, and a big, colossal waste of time.

We got her a Chromebook because a lot of what they do in middle school is more easily done with a Chromebook. They actually get a Chromebook distributed to them through the high school. So, we wanted her to have the experience of using one in middle school to get her work done.

Our son is 10. One of his favorite things is to sit and play computer games, and I can't relate to that because I've never found it fun to play video games or any of these computer games. That doesn't mean he can't do it, but I also feel like there are so many other things I would rather him do. So, we've really limited his use of the Kindle. We want him busy doing other things and being physically active, spending more time reading actual books, like the books where you turn the page.

We've never had Xbox, or DS. The only thing we bought, from a gaming standpoint, was a Wii, and that was the Christmas before last, the winter with all the snow! We got our kids Wii with winter sports games, and we got some additional games including tennis, golf and water sports. I thought it was a great way to keep them active during the winter because they could be up and moving around, pretending that they're doing these different sports. That was my whole philosophy on getting it.

I'm an older parent. I'm 52, my husband is 51. I had my daughter when I was 38 and my son when I was 41, so maybe that has something to do with how I feel about all of this. But I have this innate feeling that it's just not a productive use of time. I'm worried about where this is going and what the long-term effects are going to be of all this screen time and just sitting and staring at a screen, and maneuvering a mouse to move some character a little faster. I just don't see how that's going to get us ahead.

Colleen: It sounds to me like you've done good work in setting some boundaries at home. Let's talk more specifically about your son. You've said you don't want him on the Kindle all the time, you'd like to see him go outside more. Have you set specific boundaries for his time on the Kindle, such as no more than an hour a day, or not during the weekdays, only on weekends? Can you talk to us a little bit about those boundaries?

Nancy: Our son has been involved with running and he's been running with a team that spans from his age through high school, and they have a wonderful coach. He trains with this team several times a week. This summer, he went to Boy Scout camp - that was a sleepover camp. He also went to Camp Invention, which was really interesting. I purposely line him up for a lot of fun activities in the summer, keeping him really busy. And then when he's home, I'd love to say, "Oh, we only allow this many minutes," but really, I redirect him to other options as best as I can.

We want summer to be as much of a hiatus from screens as possible for him. When he is reading and is completely engrossed in a book and enjoying it, I feel like he is doing something productive. I want to see him that engrossed with a book, not with whatever these silly video games are.

Colleen: I get it. I like that your son takes a hiatus from screens over the summer.

Nancy: I feel if you have time to sit and play on a screen, then pick up a tennis racket and go out to the tennis courts, or go for a bike ride. Or if it's a rainy day and you don't feel like doing any of those things, I'd rather we watch a movie. See, the problem I have with a lot of this stuff, and obviously I'm not in the field like you are, but I worry about the instant gratification with games that just don't require much attention span, and I worry about how that's training the brain, and I really don't want my kids to be sucked in to all of that.

As it is, I think a lot of what they use the phone specifically for - the texting, these quick messages - they don't even have to learn how to write to text. So much is getting lost, the ability to write is almost a lost art because everything's done so quickly with a text. And then when you add in this whole focus on self... I mean, we used to use cameras to take pictures of other people. If it was your picture, you were never in it, you were taking pictures of other people. Now it's all about selfies. I'm concerned about how that's giving kids a sense of their place in the world.

It's creating a false sense of reality as well. And I think that there's a lot of stress, that having these young people, especially teenagers, so focused on what's going on between Instagram, and Snapchat, and all these different social media outlets. It's a lot of stress in their lives. They think they like it, but it seems very stressful.

Like many kids her age, our 14-year-old daughter spends time on her phone and with her starting high school, we'd like to come up with a better approach to using it. By having a phone next to you while you're studying that has social media on it, I can understand how that can be distracting. So, I suggested, "Why don't we take Instagram off your phone? You can put it on my iPad, you can have access to it any time you want, but it won't be sitting right there on your phone as a distraction. We'll put your phone on Do Not Disturb when you're studying, or you can give it to me." I was thinking of making this change when school started in September, but she took Instagram off her phone right when we talked about it and she set it up on my iPad, and that's how it's been ever since we had this conversation about two weeks ago.

She'll check Instagram from time to time, but she's not on it constantly like kids can be when it's right there on their own phone. So, I feel that was a really good move. I would not have wanted to force her to remove Instagram. I don't want her to feel out-of-the-loop, but I think that there's a compromise, and I hope we have struck the right balance.

Colleen: So, I'm going to switch to the topic of reading next. You've told me that your son loves to read Harry Potter books and that he's smart and good at that. Let's talk more about reading in your home. Do your children choose to read without prompting from a parent and/or a mandate from the school? Would they pick up a book on their own if they had free time in the day or night?

Nancy: Yes, they do. However, if I had a movie on, I don't know that my kids would take a book and go in the other room. I think it's key to provide the atmosphere that makes reading an easy choice. They like to read, once they're reading. And if it's a book that they're interested in, yes, they definitely like it and they will gravitate to the book. I get like this, and so does my husband, where you just can't put the book down, so you're trying to carve out time any chance you get to find out what's going to happen next. So yes, I do think they would pick up a book without it being a school requirement, but I find that screens, including television, are like the anti-reading. They pull kids away from reading.

And I see it with myself. I got into a bad habit of climbing into bed at night and turning on the TV. We don't watch sitcoms or reality TV, we watch the news, specifically political news shows. But news is stressful. Now, I'm trying not to turn on the news, and instead wind down by reading. I've been sleeping so much better to be honest, without looking at a screen right before I go to bed.

Colleen: Right. There is research about how screens disrupt sleep. Part of my program for parents is to help them understand that modeling reading for your kids is important. What's your take on that? Do you feel like you ever have an opportunity to read in front of your children so that you can model that reading is what adults do and it's a good and healthy choice?

Nancy: In fact, it's something my husband and I talk about a lot. We like to have books around, bookshelves where you see the books and it's easy to access them. My husband is a history buff. He's an attorney, reading is a big part of his job, and in his free time, he reads books that I would consider to be textbooks. But he's so interested and as a result, has a wealth of knowledge on these topics, and it's very interesting for the kids. He really does love to read and he models it for sure.

I like reading novels. He's more of the non-fiction reader and I'm more of the fiction reader. So yes, I do think we model it for the kids. I don't always think of it, but when I'm sitting with a book, and they see me reading, I guess you're right, that is modeling it for them. I think modeling is helpful to encourage reading.

Colleen: Do you have expectations with your kids around reading? Such as, there's a '20-minutes-a-night' rule, or 'read before bed' expectation, or 'read before screens'. Any at home boundaries that you've set?

Nancy: Well, we've tried the reading for screen time... almost like a trade. You read 15 minutes, you get 15 minutes of screen time. We tried it briefly, and then it dawned on me that I don't want to use reading as the chore and screen time as the reward. So, we backed off from that. We decided that the expectation is there will be at least 20 minutes of reading, especially for my 10-year-old son. He has to get that in at some point every night, especially during the school year. When he goes up to bed, that's when he really likes to read. He likes to get into bed after his shower and read and he ends up reading longer than 20 minutes because he gets drawn into the book, so that's great.

And our daughter, she reads a lot, partially because she needs to for school. She's always reading something. I think she does find that reading right before bed is a nice way to end the night. I tried forcing reading with the reward of screen time, and I honestly think that's not a good idea.

Colleen: Yes, I'm there with you, too. I agree with that. Some people do that, so I ask the question because it tends to be rather typical, actually. But no, you're better off not making it look like reading is the less desirable activity, because we want it to develop as a positive, lifelong habit.

Nancy: Right.

Colleen: Okay, so in my *Hooked on Screens 5 Step System*, Step 3 is to really know your child's interests well so you can support those interests. Tell me what are the kinds of things that your children are interested in? Outside of screens and outside of reading, what are some other hobbies or activities that get them excited?

Nancy: Well, they both are runners. My daughter is a cross country runner. Before she became so involved in running she was also doing ballet for many years, but you have to choose one at some point and she chose running. My son has played different sports. He's played soccer, and basketball, and baseball, but every coach has always mentioned he is a good runner, so I really think that he's probably heading in the direction of running being his predominant sport, too. They both like to play tennis, and they love our dog, Buffy, who gets lots of attention from the whole family.

But one thing that I think about often with my kids, and this plays into the whole "doing versus sitting" and looking at life on Instagram ... I had a cousin who was two years younger than me, who died of cancer when she was 32 years old. She fought cancer for about eight years. She was an amazing woman. It was a huge loss for our family when she passed, but she always had this expression, "Be a participant, not an observer." And I think of that a lot, because I think it's important to get kids to be a participant in life. Don't sit on the sidelines and watch, go play, go do, enjoy life to that level where you're actually in it. So, that's what I hope my kids will always do, just become involved. There's a time when you do need to sit back and observe, obviously when it's time to learn. But as far as extracurriculars, we tell our kids to get active and participate. It comes down to not sitting and playing tennis at a computer. Go out to the tennis courts and play real tennis! And don't watch it on TV either. Go play. It's so important for these kids to be physically active.

Colleen: Yes! So now I am going to ask you about Step 5 of my program, which is about creating adventures to help get kids excited about reading. Do you, as a family, or as a mom, plan adventures? It sounds like you do, even if you don't call them adventures. Even if it's just a day at the tennis court, or it might be something as big as a Disney World vacation. And everything in between those two experiences. My goal is to get kids to read about them first, so they become interested, and learn more about what it is you're going to go do. That way you can jump in with a higher level of knowledge and engagement. Does your family plan any kind of adventures? And if so, do you do any reading about them beforehand?

Nancy: Well one recent example would be that we wanted to try kayaking. So, we went to Wickford, Rhode Island, a lovely little town, and we rented kayaks. I rented a tandem for myself and my son, and my daughter had her own. We went kayaking around Narragansett Bay and Wickford Harbor for two hours. It was fantastic. Beautiful day. We got out there first thing in the morning, the water was flat calm.

But leading up to it, we did some research. We knew we wanted to go kayaking, we looked up the different places that we could go, there are a couple in Rhode Island; being the Ocean State we had a few options! And we also researched which type of boat, because you can rent the kind where you sit on top, or the type you sit in. We read about that so we could show up and have an idea of what we wanted to do and how to do it. So yes, we did research about it, and we had such a wonderful time. It was great!

Colleen: Do you think that your kids were - because of the research that you did - better equipped, or more excited about the adventure, because they had background knowledge that they would not have had before?

Nancy: Oh, absolutely! I think it definitely helped make them more excited, and I think they had a better idea of how to kayak too. I do think that researching and reading up together on what we were going to do really did set us up for more success that day.

Colleen: Alright. Awesome. It sounds like a super fun time. I love kayaking. Tell me about your thoughts on the use of screens in school and how much you know about that. When parents say their child only uses an hour, or two hours, or whatever their screen time use is at home, I ask them if they truly know how much screen usage is going on in school and what their opinion is on that. So, what are your thoughts on your children, their schools, and how much screens are being used there?

Nancy: Well, I totally understand how screens can be very useful in the learning process, and I feel differently about screen time as recreation versus instructional. Regardless of whether it's school or at home, I feel like some of the instructional websites are helpful for practicing math problems, for example. That, in my mind, is a productive use of time, and I don't have a problem with it. My son used to play a game called Stack the States, where he learned information about different states, the capitals, etc. And there's another game called Stack the Countries, where he learned about foreign countries.

So, when it comes to school, if they're using technology to help augment their instructional time, then I don't have a problem with that. What I would not want is kids with unsupervised time at school and access to electronics, when they could be doing something else productive. And I don't know if that happens, thankfully I haven't heard complaints about it from parents, and I haven't heard it from my kids, but that I would be against. But if they're using technology productively for instruction, or for enhancing the curriculum, then that's fine. I really think technology can be helpful in the classroom.

Colleen: Okay. As someone who studies screens and the effects on children all the way through the teen years - If you could ask me any question, what would it be?

Nancy: I do think about this concern quite a bit. What do people like you and people in your field feel the long-term effects of all this screen usage could be on these kids? From a more organic stand-point of what it's actually doing to the brain. And also, socially, how are children who are basically living their lives through screens impacted? Teenagers could be sitting around in a room with each other, not even talking, and just communicating on their phone through texting, but they're sitting together and they're not talking. I just wonder what the experts think the long-term impact of all this could be.

Nancy was spot-on with this question and we had a lengthy conversation about my thoughts and the research on it not printed here due to lack of space. However, you can read about my answers to this question, my thoughts on screen use in schools and more on my blog at www/innovativereading.com/blog.

Colleen: Nancy, it was so great to speak with you! Thank you so much for your time today. I urge everyone to go check out the great work that the BOKS program is doing at www.bokskids.org.

Parent Interview 2: Maria G. - Ridgefield, CT

Colleen: Hi Maria. Thanks so much for speaking with me today! Tell us where you live, and about your children.

Maria: I have two boys and they are 8-year-old twins. I'm a single mom and we live in Ridgefield, Connecticut.

Colleen: Wow, twins! I bet they keep you busy! OK. My first question is, do your twins use screens at home? And if they do, what kind of screens do they use and for how much time?

Maria: Yes. They use laptops a lot. They were also given iPods for gifts so they use those too. I don't know if TV is considered a screen since it is not exactly the same as a computer but they do watch TV as well.

Colleen: It is a screen. It is different than computer screens in a lot of ways, but for our purposes I still consider it a screen.

Maria: OK. That's what I thought. As far as time, it varies depending upon the day of the week and activities of the day. I try to keep it down to two hours a day. But quite honestly it could be much more than that. And weekends versus week days vary. If they have any sport or scouts or other activities that helps keep the screen time down.

And you know if I'm doing work from home then it's very difficult for me to have them not be on screens because I'm on a screen doing my work and it's hard to reason with them that this is a part of what I need to do for work. They should be doing other things or could be doing other things.

Colleen: I see how that can be hard if you are doing work at home while your kids are at home. That makes sense because they are watching what you do. You know you're making a great point because in my *Hooked on Screens 5 Step System* I talk a lot about parent modeling. We model reading and we also model screen time. That is the reality of it.

Ok so you try to set boundaries around screen time at home. You mentioned two hours. Are they hard or soft boundaries and how do you manage that?

Maria: The recommendation provided by our pediatrician was no more than two hours a day of screen time. But I find that difficult to keep. The personalities are very different between the twins and one wants to be outside playing sports while the other one is sitting in front of a computer. Then I say to the one inside, "OK you know you need to turn your computer off now." Meanwhile the other one comes in and hasn't had any screen time and he wants to watch TV. Well what am I going to say to the one who was just on the computer? Tell him to go to his room and close the door? It's so hard!

Colleen: That must be very hard. I'm sure there are a lot of parents that have similar struggles who will be relieved to hear they're not the only one having trouble keeping boundaries around screen time, especially when the children are close in age or the same age. Thanks for being honest about that.

Now let me ask you about monitoring screen time. What I mean is, do you pay attention to what the boys are doing online and give them parameters around what apps and games they can play and what social media they can visit?

Maria: They're not on any social media at this point yet since they're eight years old. They are not allowed to be on any type of game that promotes violence, but that is difficult to monitor because there are so many that use guns, or that involve capturing your opponent... So yes, I definitely do monitor that. Then I have parental controls on the computer so that adult content is filtered out. Although if you put in certain phrases or type in words that seem harmless sometimes more adult content does come up so it's not perfect.

Colleen: Right. I know parental controls are better to have than not but you still have to be vigilant as a parent and keep a close eye on what kids are doing online. So tell me why you feel the need to monitor your children's screen time.

Maria: I just don't want them to be exposed to violence unnecessarily. I don't want them to live in a bubble but for example I try not to keep the news on because the news is nothing but negative, frightening stories. Sensationalism. I feel as though the video game companies are promoting and marketing whatever sells, and violence sells in our society. But they're children, they're boys and I want them to be out enjoying nature and learning how to do things, and learning how to be social and kind and part of society and not think that being stuck to a screen is normal behavior.

I want them to have the opportunity to learn a sport, or how to play an instrument. I just think that it's not healthy for them to be interacting with a piece of electronics and not know how to interact with other people. That's a concern for me.

Colleen: Let's talk about reading next. Do either one of your two boys choose to read on their own?

Maria: Not really, to be very honest with you. But from the time they were young I have always read to them. Each one of them would choose a book that they wanted me to read. I like them to read at night before bed so we try to set the tone for that. But it's a challenge. They often want to finish a game, or get to the end of a session in a game, so it's becoming harder as they get older.

Colleen: Do you feel that the use of screens keeps your children from reading?

Maria: Yes, definitely. They definitely do, no question.

Colleen: I know you mentioned that you read to your children when they were younger. Do you have any expectations around your kids reading now?

Maria: I don't want my kids to use screens close to bedtime and we don't have a TV in their room. I prefer that the last thing they do before they go to bed is to read.

Colleen: As a parent do you have an opportunity to ever read in front of your children? I call that "modeling reading".

Maria: Right. So that is definitely a big challenge because I find most of my reading is online for work or just pleasure. But I do enjoy holding a book in my hands! Actually for the vacation we just took I purchased a book and they had the opportunity to see me actually holding the book. I read it in front of them. I never thought about that being modeling.

Although in the back of my mind I would love to have even 15-20 minutes in the evening with three comfortable chairs to sit in and have good lighting and read to ourselves. Or, if they need I would help with sounding out words and using pictures and logic to understand the words. That's my vision, the three of us being happy reading our books. Will that come to fruition? I don't know.

Colleen: Well you've got to know what you're aiming for in order to get there. Remember that when we talk about vision boards! So what are some interests your children have outside of screens and how do you support them with these interests?

Maria: Well one of my boys is very interested in sports, hockey in particular. So we did hockey all of last year and we're planning on doing it again this year. The other one expressed an interest in baseball so we just signed up for that. I changed jobs a year ago because I was working way too many hours; evenings, weekends, holidays. It was detracting from our quality of life and certainly the time I had with the boys. I changed my job so I wouldn't have those restrictions and now I'm better able to have them involved in healthy activities.

Last year I signed them up for Boy Scouts because I thought that would be something fun they would enjoy. They meet children who are not in their class at school and socialize and learn scout skills, like teamwork.

Colleen: I am sure it was a hard decision to change your job for family time and I commend you for that! Finding work-life balance can be so hard as parents.

Maria: Yes, it took me a long time to come to that decision. But I never looked back because my quality of life and being able to spend more time with the boys and support them is so worth it.

Colleen: So tell me about the books in the home that are available to your boys. What kinds of books or other reading materials do you tend to keep around?

Maria: When we go shopping if they have an interest in a magazine about cars or dogs for example we'll pick that up. I buy books for them and we go to the library and borrow books. Also, their school provides them with a level-appropriate book. Mostly it's just trying to figure out what will strike their interest.

Colleen: When I work with parents in my program, Step 4 is about taking children's interests and creating a vision board and writing in a journal to set kid-sized goals for their lives. We want kids to get excited about living life and help them see that screens are not going to get them where they want to be. But reading about their interests and goals can get them there. Have you ever kept a journal or a vision board?

Maria: That's an interesting idea. I have in the past and now it's something that is more in my head than on a piece of paper. But I do think it helps to see your goals in front of you in writing. I never thought about it like that. For the boys, if they're interested in hockey then we'll take a hockey book out of the library but not as a means to a goal that is supporting one of their interests and goals, ultimately. You know, that's a very interesting concept! I like the way that sounds.

Colleen: Great. It's part of my program and parents who work with me and follow my steps report that it completely changes their children's outlook on their hobbies as well as their understanding of the role that screens should be playing in their lives. It's powerful.

I like that you are open to embracing the idea. Let me be specific about a vision board – it's having a bulletin board that your kids can see daily and you pin up some hockey pictures, and motivational phrases, photos or images of what gets them excited in life. It's anything positive that resonates deeply with them that hangs in the home so the kids can visit often and be a reminder that to move forward on those goals screens are not going to get you there.

Maria: Wow, I think it's a great idea. When they wake up in the morning it's in front of them to remember for the day, and when they come home after school it's there too. It's not only a reminder but would be motivating for them. I love it.

Colleen: Would your children be interested if they were the ones who were keeping the vision board? If they cut out the articles and images?

Maria: They could find the pictures and the phrases, obviously with parental support, but I think that they could definitely get into it.

Colleen: The last step in my program is about planning adventures with your child and using the adventure to motivate kids to read. Let's use hockey as an example because one of your sons is interested in that. Let's say you decided to plan a trip to a pro hockey game. That is an event your one son could be excited about. That would be considered an adventure. I talk to parents about using those adventures to motivate kids to read. In this case you would read about that hockey team to learn who the players are, what are their stats, what is the history of the team, what are their strengths and weaknesses, and more.

You can also read about the rink that they play in, and about the sport of hockey in general, such as all the rules, and how it was started, where it is played professionally, etc. so when you go out to the game that adventure becomes so much more exciting because of the knowledge base that you have around it now. It really takes the fun up a few notches!

Maria: We have done that more in a generic way, such as reading about hockey in general but not before a planned event. I think reading about something that is specific and relevant to an event would be more of a motivation for them to be inquisitive and want to read. That's a great idea. It has intention behind it.

Colleen: Reading a book about hockey in general is good, because it gives you an overview of information about the game that could lead to more specific questions that kids want to know. I like to dial down to specific details because that can be fun and motivating. Can you see value in that practice? Would it resonate with your kids?

Maria: Yes definitely. Absolutely. I think that they would find that exciting and motivating.

Colleen: What advice do you have to share with parents regarding screen time?

Maria: I've noticed that when we go to the library and read there are fewer distractions! Also, it has been helpful to have other adults - relatives or family friends - read to or with my kids. That can be motivating for them. I suggest parents try both of these.

Colleen: Great recomendations. Do you have a question you'd like to ask me?

Maria: Yes I do. I wonder how I can help my boys transition from recreational screen time, when they are playing video games of their choice, to something that's more educational. No matter how many times I've tried to do this even when they were younger, it is so hard. They're very resistant. Maybe they'll start doing an educational program or game but then they quickly revert to these games with no value. It's a huge challenge, and very frustrating.

Colleen: Maria, that can be a huge frustration, I get it. Parents want their children to spend their screen time hours on quality programs and kids seem to want to choose the ones that are most exciting, entertaining and often more violent. I have some ideas for you to try on how to handle that.

Check out my blog at *www.innovativereading.com/blog* and follow me on social media where each week I answer the most popular questions that parents send in, including this question from Maria.

Parent Interview 3: Olga M. - Greenwich, CT

Colleen: Hello Olga! So glad you could chat with me today. Tell us where you live and about your children. How many do you have?

Olga: I live in Greenwich, Connecticut. I have two children, a boy who is 13 and a girl who is 8 and a half.

Colleen: Do they use screens at home, or any kind of electronic devices? If so, how long are they on screens for?

Olga: Yes, they absolutely do use screens. The both use a desktop computer, laptops and the TV. Sometimes they are on my phone in the evenings. How long they are on is embarrassing because you read everywhere that the limit should be around two hours a day. But that never happens. They never spend that little time. During the school year they'll come home after school and they'll literally get on the screens straight away. They'll change from the TV to the computer back and forth until I come home around 6:30 pm from work. So that would make it about three and a half hours for each child. Then they start homework. It could be much longer, however. On days off, like on the weekends or during the summer when they're not in camp they could literally sit in front of the screens all day if I don't physically remove them.

We are a two-parent family and I also have my mom living with us. She's the one who meets them from school. However, she is not well these days. She never enforces screen time rules. She never wants to enforce anything with them. She just spoils them. And my husband is very soft with them as well. So, the only police in the house is me and unfortunately every day when I come home I start yelling at them saying, "Shut the TV off. Get off the computer. You've been on it for too long."

Colleen: I hear your pain. You are not the only parent with this experience at home. In fact, I know many parents will take comfort in your honesty so thank you for sharing that. Tell us if you have tried to set boundaries around screen time at home.

Olga: I have tried many times to control it. Unfortunately, it's hard to control when you are not there. One of the boundaries I try to have, and sometimes it works, is no screens in the morning before school. My daughter has time before school when she has breakfast. She likes to be in the TV room and watch TV during breakfast and I don't like that. I'll say no TV - sometimes we go for a week without TV in the morning. In the evening once they do homework and then they must read there is really no time left to get back on screens anymore. But they do try!

Colleen: How about monitoring screen time? What does that look like?

Olga: I do look over it. The computer is in the office. I walk by often and pay attention to what they are on. They're mostly on YouTube watching videos. My daughter likes music videos. My son watches little kids' videos that I don't understand - all this ridiculous humor. He just likes it. I know, that's YouTube.

I also have something installed on my home computer that blocks certain content. My son uses his laptop from school so that one is in restricted mode and he cannot turn that off. When he was younger I was worried and I searched high and low to figure out how I can protect him from certain content I didn't want him to see.

Colleen: Do either of your children play any video games?

Olga: No, they don't play video games. It's just the nature of my kids. My son is just not into video games for some reason.

Colleen: That's fortunate! OK. Tell me more about what you wanted to protect them from online. Why did you feel you needed to do that?

Olga: Well I ran into a problem a few years ago where they were introduced to, or found, some adult content. They were looking at pictures and searching things out that they should not be seeing. Thankfully I don't see them doing it now. But it was very difficult to filter that out, to prevent them from accessing it. They saw how against it I was, however. I think that they just stay away from it now, as far as I know.

Colleen: OK. Wow, this is actually a common problem. Even with filters kids can find adult content on the internet today rather easily!

Olga: Yes. Like looking at porn or anything in that direction. Also hearing bad language. My daughter is exposed to some stuff I don't like even on the Disney Channel! Just the attitudes of the kids I dislike but there is no way for me to shield her from it except to just take away the TV completely. It's sad to hear it on the Disney Channel, you would think that you could trust that.

Colleen: Right!

Olga: You know I'm not from this country. I grew up in Russia in Soviet times. For me the content that's here on the Disney Channel is appalling. However, at the same time it's not like I am standing my ground, I'm allowing my child to watch these shows. But I very much dislike the attitudes. You know the girls are always mean and there's constant conflict. I didn't grow up with conflicts between girls all the time and having to be defensive. I wonder why do we show this to kids? They internalize everything. It must be a cultural difference.

Colleen: Tell us about any concerns or worries that you might have around the actual time that your kids are on screens. You mentioned that you know two hours per day is the general suggested time limit from pediatricians. What is it about your kids' time on screens that concerns you?

Olga: Transitioning them away from the screen to something else is number one. It's so hard to pull them away. It's always a fight. As a parent you have to push so hard to get them off. They'll always say, "Oh, I just want to finish this show!" or "Just let me finish this video." So another five or ten minutes go by and it repeats itself. Another concern is the way their brain develops and they no longer have the attention span for quiet activities and for reading and for thinking or processing information…it all concerns me. Again, I don't really have a good backbone at home and the other adults here don't support me in enforcing the limits. It's hard. I find myself fighting uphill every single day.

Colleen: Do you notice if it changes your children's personality or temperament after screen use? I've had parents tell me that, so I'm curious what your thoughts are.

Olga: Absolutely! They're more stimulated, awake. And it also brings them down emotionally. I have an example of how reading has the opposite effect though, from just last night. My daughter was so tired and having a bad night. Everything was wrong and she was yelling, so finally I said, "Let's just read a book for 15 minutes and you will feel a lot better." And that's exactly what happened. Then I opened your website on my phone and I read that you say exactly that! I said to myself, "Why haven't I thought of this before?" I really should think about reading in that way - that reading is calming. It truly helped my daughter calm down.

Colleen: I'm so glad you found my website helpful. Excellent.

Olga: Oh yes.

Colleen: Great! So, do your children ever choose to read on their own?

Olga: That's a good question. When my son was little we used to read to him all the time. At three years old he had the attention span to listen to *The Cat In the Hat*. It's a long book! We have such fond memories of reading at night - both my husband and me - and enacting all the scenes. It was great! Later on, even though he struggled with reading in school I still pushed it at home and I still read with him. He would read a paragraph and I would read a paragraph.

However now he doesn't read on his own routinely, and not until this past summer would he choose to pick up a book - there were only a couple of times where he would read on his own desire without me telling him to read. He loved *Diary of a Wimpy Kid*!

I worried all the time that he didn't read for pleasure. He always read because he was told to read. Finally, he became interested in Harry Potter. I pushed that and he listened to the audio books - we started listening to it in the car. He got interested and then he got hooked. He went home that same day and he listened for another hour and now he's on the fourth book. Unfortunately, he's still not reading it by himself. He is listening to the audio book and following in the book. But he follows it every word! Still, screens come first in his mind.

Colleen: That's wonderful! That's a great story. There is nothing wrong with listening to the audiobook and reading along with it, especially for struggling or disengaged readers.

Olga: I'm really hoping that this will start him on the road to reading for pleasure. For my daughter, she does not read for pleasure. She does not pick up a book by herself. She only reads when I tell her she must. We also struggle to find books she will like.

Colleen: Do you think that the use of screens keeps your children from reading?

Olga: Yes! I believe that screens are taking away a lot of time that could be spent reading. Also, they provide the constant entertainment that kids crave. Right now kids get just about all of their entertainment from screens. They don't want to do anything, they just turn the TV on or the computer on and it's all right there. Books are a lot more work. They have to use their imagination with books.

Colleen: You're right. Do you have any expectations around reading for your kids at home?

Olga: The school assigns reading as part of their homework. For my older one it's half an hour and for my younger one it's 20 minutes per night. Some parents have increased that time and they have the older ones read for 45 minutes. I just stick to what the school says and we get it in usually 5 nights a week.

Colleen: As a parent do you ever have an opportunity to read in front of your children?

Olga: I do read books myself but it's usually on the train to work. They don't see me read often. I read at home on my phone but that's on a screen... But I'm reading and not watching videos. I do read, even though maybe they don't see it that often. Now my husband, however, he's a big reader and he literally spends his days off sitting in a room where we don't have any screens and just reads and reads for hours on end! They also see their grandparents read.

Colleen: OK. Then you must have books in the home. Where do you keep them?

Olga: We have plenty of books in the home. We have a bunch in our bedroom. There is a whole wall in the family room even though there might be books that kids are not going to look at. Kids' books are in my son's room and in the office.

Colleen: OK great. Does your daughter have books in her room too?

Olga: She has a few. Her room is very small and doesn't have a shelf so there are a few books on her doll house. Her room used to have a box of baby books when she was little.

Colleen: So what other activities are your children interested in?

Olga: My son is a Boy Scout. Both do karate. And my daughter plays piano.

Colleen: They have other interests then, that's wonderful. Which leads me to ask you about your thoughts on Step 5 in my program which is planning family adventures and reading about the event beforehand. How would your children respond to that?

Olga: I think it's a great idea! I planned a whole Disney vacation last year by myself, however I did tell the kids about it. My son is savvy around the internet so he does research. But again, he would do it on YouTube and he would watch a video instead of reading. I think it's a great idea because you need to teach kids to look at different sources and not trust just one source. You can allow them to watch a video but you then you have to say, "OK, now you also have to look at this book and read this other resource." Yeah, I think that's wonderful.

Colleen: I like that – it's an integrated approach for kids who are real video-watchers! You could start with 1-2 videos as a warm-up and then let that lead to 1 guidebook, 1 magazine and a few pamphlets and maps to round out the collection of information.

Do you know how much screen time your kids get during the school day? In other words, how many hours a day do you think your kids might be on screens at school, and does that concern you at all?

Olga: It does concern me because it all started with my son two years ago when the elementary school gave him an iPad. They gave an iPad to every single kid in the school system - their own iPad! My son could bring that iPad home every day starting in fourth grade. They have educational apps and he could read on it. He'd also record videos on it. He's creative, but it's still screen time. So my concern is just that.

School provides this device and my kids come home and they're not really under strict supervision. There is no way for me to physically take away the device. They have this in their hands until I come home and physically remove it. Then he has to do homework and it's on the computer again.

Colleen: OK thank you for articulating that so well. I appreciate you sharing that. Many districts are giving devices to students these days for educational purposes, starting in elementary school. This practice has both upsides and downsides for sure. Do you have any other concerns regarding screens I haven't asked about?

Olga: In reading your articles online I saw you wrote about how yelling and screaming doesn't work. It's not pleasant but I do eventually get my kids off the screens like that. But nobody likes doing it that way and it's the same problem every night! I find it helpful when I read about other methods. I want to know exactly what phrases to use so I don't have to yell. What can I say to my kids that will work? I always like when authors give examples or phrases for parents to use for kids.

Colleen: I totally get it which is why in every blog article I give parents a free download with the exact method I write about. In the article on not yelling, I provide a link to a free download on exactly what to say to kids that works to get them off screens instead! I'll send you the link.

Olga: Oh that's great! Thank you!

Colleen: Thank you so much for sharing your story with parents!

Get my free download: **15 Phrases to Say to Your Child to Get Him to Read Without Threatening, Nagging or Yelling!** http://bit.ly/nonagging

Parents' Words of Wisdom:

In my work with parents at Innovative Reading, I talk to parents every day who are dealing with kids and screen time at home. Here are some of their struggles, ideas, and thoughts on the issue:

"I think a lot of times what the child would prefer in lieu of a screen is just their parent's presence. So that can go a long way to pulling back screen time." Jen W.

"No video games are allowed at all during the week. Weekends are more relaxed but I keep my kids busy. Music practice, sports, chores. If they can do it all and find time for video games or a movie, they're welcome to relax. But no idling about until everything else is handled." Natasha Z.

"I make sure to schedule activities daily during the summer and weekends - even when I am busy. My daughter has quite a few craft kits and games to play on her own. But I also think you have to be intentional when it comes to the topic of screens." Malla H.

"This is a problem I am having right now with my 8-year-old. I am getting worried that he has no interests and would pick the iPad over everything else if he could. We are a busy family and he enjoys our activities but he has no interest in anything else when we get home. I think I have to go cold turkey and take it away completely." Maybelline T.

"We don't allow much screen time in our house (our girls are 7 & 3). They read, play board games or do arts & crafts. My older one is involved in Girl Scouts and sports so we keep her busy with that." Erin M.

"I am having a real issue. My 5-year-old daughter is definitely addicted. The other activities she enjoys are sensory things such as making homemade slime, Play Doh, playing with water and role playing. She'd much rather be on screens though." Jazilyn F.

"Kids need to be kept busy. Parent involvement is key. You need parents to be willing to not only take kids to practice and games, but to volunteer as a coach." Tiz N.

"I don't allow cell phones for kids or adults at meals. I go through my kids' social media accounts until they are old enough to pay for their own phones. I turn all apps off at 9 pm and all internet off at 10 pm for my 15-year-old and 11 pm for my 17-year-old. They do not complain." Connie D.

"We have had a drying-out period in our home recently, because our son was starting to worry my husband and me. We really felt like he was heading towards addiction with how he wanted to spend so much of his time on screens. We agreed it required quitting cold turkey, and so we decided this summer was going to be screen-less." Nancy S.

"I'm much stricter about things than my husband and it can often be exhausting keeping everyone on task. But I've seen the alternative - our oldest once logged nearly 12 hours in one day on a video game console. I turned on all the parental controls at that point." Natasha Z.

More Support
- Ready to Go All-In?

I wrote this book because I know my *Hooked on Screens 5 Step System* works. I have used these steps with parents for the past 20 years as an educator and watched them work for kids as young as 3-years-old all the way through high school. Now, for the first time, these steps are available in a book. I am sure your family will benefit if you choose to implement the strategies and stay consistent.

If you would like more targeted support with implementing this program, or if you feel your child has a screen addiction and you would benefit from 1:1 coaching with me, please contact me at colleen@innovativereading.com to discuss how I can further support your family.

If anyone in your family has a serious screen addiction, it won't go away on its own. Reach out today for help. See my **Resources** page for options.

Resources

Short reading material suggestions: for reading to/with kids, or parent modeling (they are fast, fun and interesting! Best of all you can finish them quickly):

Poetry for kids to read, or for read alouds – Try authors such as Roald Dahl, Nikki Giovanni, Jack Prelutzky, Dr. Seuss, Shel Silverstein

Poetry for **grown-ups** (especially for modeling) – Try authors such as Maya Angelou, Edgar Allen Poe, Emily Dickenson, Ernest Hemingway, Rumi, Walt Whitman

Collections of short stories suitable for **grown-ups**: Try the following recommendations by www.Goodreads.com: *Interpreter of Maladies* by Jhumpa Lahiri, *That Glimpse of Truth* edited by David Miller, *The Thing Around Your Neck* by Chimamanda Ngozi Adichie and *Tenth of December* by George Saunders

Super short books for **grown-ups**: *Poke the Box* by Seth Godin, *Lifeboat No. 8* by Elizabeth Kaye, *Very Good Lives* by J.K. Rowling, *Smile* by Ron Gutman, *The Case of the Caretaker* by Agatha Christie

Journaling and vision boards:

The 5 Minute Journal https://www.intelligentchange.com/products/the-five-minute-journal

Places to get inspiration or materials for vision boards:

Search: Vision boards on Etsy, Pinterest, Google Images, Amazon

Ideas for family day trip adventures:

Local, state and national parks – look for guided day hikes, birding walks, cross-country skiing or snowshoeing tours, leaf and tree identification walks, Civil and Revolutionary War reenactments, and more

History and art museums, aquariums, science and space centers

Art shows, galleries, sculpture walks or gardens

Visit the firehouse, police station, local courthouse, a town monument, historic burial site, or any place that represents local history, civics or politics

Watch a competition sport (local, college, national, international): Baseball parks, football games, hockey games, lacrosse games, chess tournaments, sailboat or crew racing

Take a lesson in a new sport: kayaking, horseback riding, ping pong, badminton, ultimate frisbee, golf, tennis, rock climbing, swimming

Take a lesson in something fun: stand-up comedy, acting, tango, jewelry making, creative writing, Zumba, basket weaving, Mexican cooking, cake decorating, face painting, yoga

Book conventions (Like Bookcon)

Local, high school, college, Broadway or off-Broadway musicals, plays or other theater or dance performances

Spend time with animals: Visit a county fair, animal shelter, local farm, animal sanctuary, apiary, petting zoo, butterfly house, wildlife preservation area, reptile sanctuary, nature center, aquarium

Spend time in nature: take a hike (and bring a wildflower identification book), ride bikes at the park in autumn to enjoy the leaves, walk a trail and look for scats and tracks (bring an identification book), swim in the creek and look for fish, find a bike path and take a ride, walk the shore of an ocean, lake, pond or river and make observations

Volunteer: senior centers, animal shelters (read to the dogs and cats!), children's hospitals, homeless shelters, food collection sites, write to the troops, donate presents to children for the holidays, participate in a youth group, box up gently used clothing and drop off to charity, participate in a clothes or food drive, participate in a walk-a-thon or kids race, donate your gently used books to make room for more, learn a craft and make items to donate (knitting, sewing, crocheting, cooking)

Food delivery or meal prep services - This list could be endless. Search for apps, local restaurant delivery services and check your local grocery store to see if they deliver. Many of them do:

www.plated.com
www.hellofresh.com
www.butcherbox.com
www.grubhub.com
www.blueapron.com
www.greenchef.com - gluten free

Non-smartphone calling devices:

Gizmo Gadget, Gizmo Pal 2

For tracking and monitoring screen time:

Moment Family (iOS)
unGlue (iOS)
Bosco (iOS and Android)
Bark (iOS and Android)
Circle by Disney (iOS and Android)
ScreenTime (iOS, Amazon, Android)

For screen addiction:

www.NetAddiction.com – Information on internet and screen addiction, treatment, counseling and more

www.GameQuitters.com – A support site for people and their families overcoming gaming addiction, founded by Cam Adair, recovered gamer

www.cgaa.info – A support group for computer gaming addicts and their families

www.innovativereading.com - my website for helping families win the battle of screen time and replace it with healthy activities such as reading. I also offer group and 1:1 coaching programs for parents

Acknowledgments

I have been an avid reader all my life. These days I can be found reading in my office as early as 5 am, with a cup of tea in hand and my journal by my side. My genre of choice Monday – Friday is non-fiction, usually about business or literacy, with a few other topics such as faith, spirituality and health mixed in. Weekends I start a little later, maybe 8 am. I lean more towards magazines than books on Saturday and Sunday, and meet my husband in the sun room (again, with my tea!) where he reads the news and the Bible. We both agree this reading ritual is the highlight of each day and have been doing it for years.

A decade ago I was more of a fiction fan. I found authors I loved and read every book each one wrote. I found fiction stories set in a historical context the most riveting, and would get lost in books such as *The Girl with a Pearl Earring*, and *The Secret Life of Bees*. Each book would increase my interest in that time period and I'd have to go hunting for more titles set in the same era. The very act of reading books fueled my passion for learning, and therefore reading more books. This was evident in my adulthood for sure, though it began in my childhood in grade school.

I can remember my elementary years vividly by the books I read and the characters that fascinated me through the pages. I was a fiction fan as a child, and went through waves of interest from historical fiction, to realistic fiction to fantasy and then eventually mystery. I most recall the incredible excitement of "getting back to my book" if I had to put it down to go eat or be forced to go to sleep! How hard that was when I had such strong female protagonists waiting for me such as Pippi

Longstocking (*The Adventures of Pippi Longstocking*), Laura Ingalls Wilder (*The Little House Series*), Miss Eglantine Price (*Bedknobs and Broomsticks*), Lucy Penvensie (*The Lion, the Witch and the Wardrobe*), and Nancy Drew (*The Nancy Drew Mystery Series)*. These books shaped my childhood and my life passions to this very day and are the reason I do what I do now.

Today, I thank the authors who dreamed up these characters and created the fiction stories, or who lived the stories and dared to tell their life experiences. Thank you for writing incredibly fascinating, hysterically funny and highly adventurous books that took me around the world from my small suburban bedroom in Westchester County, New York. I developed an imagination and many ideas that may never have come to fruition without the inspiration from authors before me who were willing to tell stories and share their knowledge. I have been benefitting from authors ever since and I hope that my work now inspires others.

Thank you, mom and dad, who always promoted reading in our home and who ensured, through treks to the public library no matter the weather, that my sisters and I had plenty of reading material at all times.

Thank you to my husband, Dan, for sharing your love of reading spiritual books with me and for supporting me in writing a book of my own. I enjoy every weekend moment we spend reading in each other's company.

Thank you to friend and mastermind partner, Jonathan Christian, for writing the foreword to this book as a social media strategist and expert; sharing with readers the perspective of how screens and the online world can be beneficial when used appropriately.

Thank you to Nancy D., Maria G. and Olga M. for their time and honesty during our interviews to share real-life experiences of parents in the trenches with screens at home every day.

Thank you to the thousands of parents who subscribe to my email newsletter, try my strategies and share success stories of their children putting down screens and picking up books. I applaud all of you who come out to my talks and workshops and go home and implement what you learned right away. Additional thanks to the growing number of parents working with me 1:1 in my *Hooked on Screens 5 Step System* to realize amazing off-screen gains with their children. Bravo to all of you! Your commitment is truly validated by the success of your children.

Thank you to parents everywhere who believe that their children deserve to grow and flourish to their maximum potential and who see reading as a key tool to help them do just that.

Glossary of (Obvious and Not So Obvious) Terms Used in This Book

Boundary – the limit you set around screen time

Electronic devices – Any and all computers and tech gadgets, also known as screens

Ereader – A device used mostly for reading, such as a Kindle or Nook

Modeling – Setting an example by displaying a behavior that another person follows

Monitor – To watch closely, to oversee or to supervise

Recreational screen time – The time spent on electronic devices that is not homework or schoolwork related. I include educational games because even though some may help with learning, they are still games by definition and therefore many of the same effects of screen use still apply

Screens – Another word for any form of electronic device with a viewing window, such as smartphones, tablets, laptop computers, desk top computers, video game consoles, ereaders, handheld devices and televisions

Tablet – A thin, portable, touchscreen computer without an attached keyboard. The most popular example to date is the iPad

'**Tween** – A youth in the pre-teen years between the ages of 10 and 12, not still a little child but not yet a teen

Video game – a game played by manipulating images produced by a computer program on a screen. Popular examples today are Minecraft, World of Warcraft, Grand Theft Auto, Tetris

Video game console – A computer machine primarily designed for use to play video games

Book Dr. Colleen Carroll to Speak

Book Dr. Colleen Carroll as your keynote speaker!

As your keynote, Dr. Carroll will ensure your event is motivating, inspiring, educational and transformational

Consider her for your next conference, workshop or event:

- School districts/private schools and academies/educational groups/PTAs/PTOs
- Pediatricians, neurologists
- Child psychiatrists, psychologists, counselors and social workers
- Homeschoolers
- Parenting groups and organizations

For over two decades, Dr. Carroll has been educating and motivating parents, teachers and administrators with her inspiring take on literacy and in particular, how to help parents create and keep a Reader-Friendly Home™. Her mission is to ensure that all children grow up in a home where reading is valued and practiced. This gives every child, regardless of their background or economic situation, an opportunity to succeed in the world because they are a strong reader and have gained experience and knowledge through the written word.

Since the boom in youth screen use, Dr. Carroll has researched the impact on children. She created her company, Innovative Reading, to help parents monitor and set boundaries around screen time at home to protect their children and stop screen addiction before it happens.

To date, Dr. Carroll has touched thousands of families internationally through her blog at www.InnovativeReading.com/blog, and through podcast interviews, magazine and journal articles, as well as speaking at conferences and workshops.

Her unique strategies offer parents a realistic and doable no-nonsense approach that holds all family members accountable for children's success in reading by getting control of the screens at home. Dr. Carroll speaks on this topic and more in a humorous, interesting manner and leaves the audience excited to put her ideas into practice.

For more information on how to book Dr. Carroll for a speaking event, professional development workshop or media interview, email drcarroll@innovativereading.com.

CPSIA information can be obtained
at www.ICGtesting.com
Printed in the USA
FFOW01n1215240318
45864835-46762FF

9 780692 939093